. . . .

THE NEW GLOBAL ECONOMY

AND DEVELOPING COUNTRIES:

MAKING OPENNESS WORK

D1111520

POLICY ESSAY NO. 24

THE NEW GLOBAL ECONOMY

AND DEVELOPING COUNTRIES:

MAKING OPENNESS WORK

DANI RODRIK

DISTRIBUTED BY THE
JOHNS HOPKINS UNIVERSITY PRESS

PUBLISHED BY THE
OVERSEAS DEVELOPMENT COUNCIL
WASHINGTON, DC

Copyright © 1999 by Overseas Development Council, Washington, DC

Distributed by:
    The Johns Hopkins University Press
    2715 North Charles Street
    Baltimore, MD 21218-4319

Library of Congress Cataloging-In-Publication Data

Rodrik, Dani
    The New Global Economy and Developing Countries: Making Openness Work/Dani Rodrik

p.   cm.   (Policy Essay: No. 24)
Includes bibliographic references.
        1. Developing countries—Foreign economic relations.   2. International economic relations.   3. Free trade.   4. Competition, International.   I. Title   II. Series.

HF1413.R62   1999   337'.09172'4—dc21   98–54766   CIP

ISBN: 1-56517-027-X

Printed in the United States of America.
Publications Editor: Jacqueline Edlund-Braun
Edited by Vincent Ercolano
Cover design: Design Consultants of Virginia

The views expressed in this volume are those of the author and do not necessarily represent those of the Overseas Development Council as an organization or of its individual officers, Board, Council, Program Associates Group, advisory groups, and staff members.

Contents

Foreword

The Asian financial crisis brought home to many people in both developed and developing countries the realities of promoting development in a globalized economy. Now the key concern of policymakers and the public is how to deal with the forces of *globalization*—the whirlwind of technological change and liberalized trade and investment that is bringing huge gains in communications and efficiency, and effecting huge shifts in wealth and production.

Globalization is a fact of life. The issue is how policymakers in all countries deal with it. On balance, globalization has brought great benefits. Increased trade and capital flows have generated gains in productivity and efficiency that have spurred growth and created millions of jobs in the advanced industrial countries, the emerging economies, and even many of the world's low-income countries. But while globalization has opened up vast new opportunities for economic and social progress, it also has brought costs. These costs include instabilities, as we have witnessed in Asia over the past year, and marginalization of countries and individuals not equipped to take advantage of globalization's opportunities. If globalization is not managed wisely, these costs will increase.

In this new world economy, development remains critically important. Despite economic and social progress over the last 40 years, much remains to be done. The number of people living in absolute poverty is still far too high and likely to increase in the next few years, and the gap between rich and poor nations is widening. Furthermore, both rich and poor countries face a set of common problems—environmental degradation, new and old diseases, crime, and drug trafficking—that must be addressed collectively.

From a development perspective, the key challenge for decision makers is to design and adopt a set of policies that will ensure their countries can seize the opportunities created by globalization, so that people—and particularly poor people—can benefit from integration into the globalized economy, while at the same time can be protected from the inevitable costs that flow from rapid economic, social, and political change.

In that regard, the key question now being debated by policy makers and scholars is how quickly developing countries should open their economies to unrestricted flows of trade and investment in order to promote economic growth. In this Policy Essay, *Making Openness Work: The New Global Economy and the Developing Countries*, Dani Rodrik, Rafiq Hariri Professor of International Political Economy at Harvard University and Senior Advisor to ODC, addresses that important question. Dr. Rodrik provides an empirical analysis that will contribute to deepening and clarifying that debate. He argues that there is no evidence to back the claims of many that integration into the global economy *in and of itself* will improve economic performance. Indeed, according to Rodrik's analysis, there is no convincing evidence that openness, in the sense of low barriers to trade and capital flows systematically produces [economic growth]. In practice the links between openness and economic growth tend to be weak, and to be contingent on the presence of complementary policies and institutions. (p. 137)

He recommends that developing countries:

> need to create an environment that is conducive to private investment . . . . They need to improve their institutions of conflict management—legally guaranteed civil liberties and political freedoms, social partnerships, and social insurance—so that they can maintain macroeconomic stability and adjust to rapid changes in external circumstances. In the absence of these complements to a strategy of external liberalization, openness will not yield much. At worst, it will cause instability widening inequalities and social conflict. (p. 137)

In other words, openness will not work in the absence of an effective participatory domestic *development* strategy. It requires a complementary set of domestic policies and institutions.

Making Openness Work is a product of ODC's program on *globalization, equity, and development.* This program rests on the proposition that the integration of the national economies into the world economy is *the* major dynamic of our time, and that this process poses opportunities and risks for developing as well as developed countries. The opportunities include the improved prospect for eradicating global poverty in the first decades of the next century and the potential for building new international partnerships to achieve sustainable development on a global scale. The risks include heightened economic insecurity and inequality (and social exclusion) and political instability, with uncertain consequences for democracy and social harmony. New and creative policies and partnerships will be required if the benefits of globalization are to be maximized and the risks minimized. And that in turn will require the building of consensus on values and policy options, as well as institutional and democratic reforms of the current multilateral system. ODC's program is designed to contribute to those ends.

This Policy Essay results from ODC's overall program of research and analysis on multilateral cooperation for development, which was made possible by the generous funding of The Ford Foundation and the Rockefeller Foundation. We are grateful for their support and encouragement.

John W. Sewell
ODC President
January 1999

Acknowledgments

This essay would not have been written without the encouragement and support of Catherine Gwin and John Sewell of the Overseas Development Council. I thank them both, as well as Michael McDowell (also of the ODC), for their advice and guidance.

Along with Catherine Gwin and John Sewell, many other individuals made comments that substantially improved the manuscript. I thank in particular Paul Collier, Susan Collins, Avinash Dixit, David Gordon, Gerry Helleiner, Joan Nelson, Dave Richardson, James Rauch, James Robinson, Jonathan Temple, Nicolas van de Walle, and Adrian Wood, most of whom provided detailed written comments. In addition, I have benefited from numerous conversations with my colleagues Robert Lawrence and Ray Vernon, who have helped me sort out my ideas. Needless to say, none of these individuals should be held responsible for the views expressed herein. I also thank the Division for International Development Cooperation of the Ministry for Foreign Affairs, Sweden, for permission to use some of the research originally commissioned by them (Rodrik 1997c).

Research assistance along the way from Vladimir Kliouev, Chad Steinberg, and Joanna Veltri has been indispensable. Joanna Veltri, in particular, made key contributions to this project, ranging from significant editorial improvements to background research.

Executive Summary

The process of global economic integration has sharply altered the context in which most governments are thinking about policies for economic development. The world economy and the "dictates" of international economic integration loom much larger than ever before. Indeed, in many "emerging" economies traditional developmental concerns relating to industrialization and poverty have been crowded out by the pursuit of "international competitiveness."

Openness to the world economy can be a source of many economic benefits. The importation of investment and intermediate goods that may not be available domestically at comparable cost, the transfer of ideas and technology from more developed nations, and access to foreign savings can help poor nations circumvent some of the traditional obstacles to rapid growth. But these are only *potential* benefits, to be realized in full only when the complementary policies and institutions are in place domestically.

The claims made by the boosters of international economic integration are frequently inflated or downright false. Countries that have done well in the postwar period are those that have been able to formulate a domestic investment strategy to kick-start growth and those that have had the appropriate institutions to handle adverse external shocks, not those that have relied on reduced barriers to trade and capital flows. The evidence from the experience of the last two decades is quite clear: the countries that have grown most rapidly since the mid-1970s are those that have invested a high share of GDP and maintained macroeconomic stability. The relationship between growth rates and indicators of openness—levels of tariff and nontariff barriers or controls on capital flows—is weak at best. Policymakers therefore have to focus on the fundamentals of economic growth—investment, macroeconomic stability, human resources, and good governance—and not let international economic integration dominate their thinking on development.

AN INVESTMENT STRATEGY

■ IN THE LONG RUN, INVESTMENT IS KEY to economic performance. Recent studies on the sources of East Asian growth have highlighted the overwhelming importance of accumulation for the countries in that region. While opening up to the world economy can sometimes stimulate investment, it is a mistake to believe that there is a determinate relationship between openness and investment levels. Governments in East Asia complemented their outward-orientation with a coherent domestic investment strategy that raised the private return to capital and kindled the animal spirits of entrepreneurs.

There is no single way of raising the private return to capital to start this process. Even among the East Asian cases, investment subsidies took different forms. Governments have to be imaginative in devising investment strategies that exploit their countries' resources and capabilities, while respecting administrative and budgetary constraints. A useful starting point is to acknowledge that openness is *part* of a development strategy; it does not substitute for it.

STRENGTHENING INSTITUTIONS OF CONFLICT MANAGEMENT

■ THE ABILITY TO MAINTAIN MACROECONOMIC STABILITY in the face of turbulent external conditions is the single most important factor accounting for the diversity in post-1975 economic performance in the developing world. The countries that were unable to adjust their macroeconomic policies to the shocks of the late 1970s and early 1980s ended up experiencing a dramatic collapse in productivity growth.

The countries that fell apart did so because their social and political institutions were inadequate to bring about the bargains required for macroeconomic adjustment—they were societies with weak institutions of conflict management. In the absence of institutions that mediate conflict among social groups, the policy adjustments needed to re-establish macroeconomic balance are delayed, as labor, business, and other social groups block the implementation of fiscal and exchange-rate policies. The result is that the economy finds itself confronted with high inflation, scarcity of foreign currency, and a myriad of other bottlenecks.

Societies with deeper cleavages (along ethnic, income, or regional lines) are particularly susceptible to policy paralysis of this sort, making institutions of conflict management all the more important in such societies. Evidence shows that participatory political institutions, civil and political liberties, high-quality bureaucracies, the rule of law, and mechanisms of social insurance such as social safety nets can bridge these cleavages. These institutions are important both for managing turbulence in the world economy and for countering the possible widening of inequality that openness can bring.

· ·

IMPLICATIONS FOR INTERNATIONAL GOVERNANCE

■ IT IS NOT REALISTIC TO EXPECT THAT national development efforts will converge on a single model of "good economic behavior"; nor is it desirable that they do so. The lesson of history is that ultimately all successful countries develop their own brands of national capitalism. The economies that have done well in the postwar period have all succeeded via their own particular brand of heterodox policies. Macroeconomic stability and high investment rates have been common, but beyond that many details have differed. Correspondingly, the rules of the international economy must be flexible enough to allow individual developing countries to develop their own "styles" of capitalism, in the same way that countries such as Japan, Germany, and the United States have in the past evolved their own different models.

· ·

CONCLUSION

■ DEVELOPMENT POLICY IS PRONE TO FASHIONS. During the 1950s and 1960s, when import-substitution was in vogue, there was excessive optimism about what government interventions could achieve. Now that outward-orientation is the norm, there is excessive faith in what openness can accomplish. Early on, planning models emphasized capital accumulation at the expense of price incentives and the role of markets. Today the importance of investment is consistently downplayed. The swing of the pendulum from one extreme to another creates blind spots, risking yet another unproductive change in fashions.

The internationalization of production and investment raises a fundamental question of accountability: to whom will national economic policymakers be accountable? The implicit answer provided by the globalization model is that they will be accountable to foreign investors, country-fund managers in London and New York, and a relatively small group of domestic exporters. In the globalized economy, these are the groups that determine whether an economy is judged a success or not, and whether it will prosper.

This would not necessarily be a bad thing if the invisible hand of global markets could always be relied on to produce desirable outcomes. The reality is considerably more murky. It takes too much blind faith in markets to believe that the global allocation of resources is enhanced by the twenty-something-year-olds in London who move hundreds of millions of dollars around the globe in a matter of an instant, or by the executives of multinational enterprises who make plant-location decisions on the basis of the concessions they can extract from governments.

Consequently, governments and policy advisors alike have to stop thinking of international economic integration as an end in itself. Developing nations have to engage the world economy on their own terms, not on terms set by global markets or multilateral institutions.

Chapter 1
Introduction

A DAY IN THE LIFE OF A FINANCE MINISTER

■   THE FINANCE MINISTER BEGINS HIS DAY BY LOGGING ON to his computer to find out how currency and equity markets have been doing in the United States, Europe, and East Asia. He searches the Internet for press reports and leafs through the international financial press on his desk. The international markets are calm, and his search turns up no unpleasant news items on his country's economy. Relieved, he postpones the decision he had made the night before to raise interest rates.

An assistant has circled an item in the *Financial Times* on U.S. plans to bring the government of a neighboring country before the World Trade Organization (WTO) on the grounds that this country's regional assistance programs violate trade rules. The minister makes a mental note to check with the minister of trade and industry to see whether their country's own regional policies can be challenged in the WTO as well.

The first meeting of the day is a staff briefing on the upcoming consultation with the International Monetary Fund (IMF). The IMF has been complaining that the country's fiscal deficit remains too high and that its social security system needs an overhaul. The minister tells his staff to prepare a new set of budget projections based on smaller public-sector wage increases for the coming year.

A delegation from an international credit-rating agency is ushered in next. The minister gives his standard speech. The economy has been transformed in the last few years and is poised for takeoff. Exports are up 15 percent, the main state-owned petroleum firm is about to be privatized, and the fallout in the stock market from the Asian financial crisis has been contained so far. The government remains more committed than ever to responsible financial and fiscal policies. One of the members of the delegation, introduced as the new desk economist for the country, is furiously taking notes. The minister notices that he does not look any older than his own son, who has just graduated from college and whom he considers barely responsible enough to be entrusted with the family car.

At lunch, the minister is a keynote speaker at a conference put together by a major international consulting firm on "The Imperatives of Globalization." "We are all globalizers now," he concludes to applause. "No nation can afford to stay outside the mainstream of the global economy. We must make our economies internationally competitive by opening up, liberalizing, and privatizing. Only then can we generate employment and growth opportunities for our economies."

In the afternoon, the minister meets first with a group of businessmen representing his country's largest exporting firms. The delegation complains about the level of the exchange rate. Its members are worried that the government's policy of high interest rates is keeping the domestic currency too strong, and that their products are being priced out of competition in world markets. The minister promises to expand the range of tax credits for which exporters can qualify.

Next in line is the chief executive of a prominent international energy firm, accompanied by a former U.S. secretary of defense. The executive reiterates his company's strong interest in the forthcoming privatization of the national oil company. The former defense secretary underlines the importance of the country to the United States and emphasizes that the auctioning of the oil company will be watched closely as a signal of the country's determination to join "the civilized world of free-market economies." The minister reminds himself to read a report recently prepared by the antitrust commission on the consequences of the monopolization of the energy sector.

After another check of international financial markets and a quick update of the news on CNN, the minister is ready to go home. As he is leaving, he becomes vaguely aware of the din outside the ministry building. His aide apologizes, saying that it has proved difficult to keep away the public employees who have been demonstrating for days for their back pay. The minister sighs. He hopes he can make it home in time for his favorite TV show, *The X-Files*.

. . . .

THE NEW GLOBAL ENVIRONMENT
FOR DEVELOPMENT

■ PRIOR TO THE RECENT BLOWUP IN GLOBAL FINANCIAL MARKETS, this could have been a typical day in the life of a finance minister in Brazil, Russia, Turkey, or any of the scores of developing countries that were fast becoming integrated into the world economy. In all such countries, the context in which governments are thinking about policies for economic development, and the terms around which such policies are discussed, have changed radically. The world economy and the "dictates" of international economic integration loom much larger than ever before. Policymakers have become all too aware of the increasing attention that their national economies' relations with foreign markets demand. As Table 1.1 shows, the volume of international trade increased at twice the rate of growth of world output from 1985 to 1994. Gross capital flows expanded even more dramatically, increasing at double-digit rates annually.

International economic integration is driven partly by technological changes that have reduced transport and communications costs. But the progressive removal of restrictions on trade in goods, services, and capital has also played an important role. In this new environment, external constraints on the exercise of fiscal, monetary, trade, and industrial policies have become considerably tighter. International capital markets are quick to punish countries that pursue policies that are perceived to be incompatible with macroeconomic sustainability. The ubiquitous role of the World Bank and the IMF make it harder for governments dependent on these institutions to embark on economic strategies that depart from orthodoxy. The new disciplines negotiated during the Uruguay Round of trade negotiations impose additional restrictions on trade and industrial policies, as in the case of domestic content requirements or patent laws. In addition, many developing countries are under pressure from nongovernmental organizations in the Northern Hemisphere to raise labor and environmental standards.

TABLE 1.1. GROWTH OF INTERNATIONAL ECONOMIC ACTIVITY, 1964-1994 (annual averages, in percent)

	Export Volume	World DFI Flows	International Bank Loans	World Real GDP
1964-1973	9.2	—	34.0	4.6
1973-1980	4.6	14.8	26.7	3.6
1980-1985	2.4	4.9	12.0	2.6
1985-1994	6.7	14.3	12.0	3.2

Source: Rowthorn and Kozul-Wright (1998) from original IMF and BIS sources.
Note: DFI: direct foreign investment.

Partly as a consequence of the conditionality imposed by the World Bank and the IMF, but also because of widespread domestic dissatisfaction with the previous set of import-substitution policies, outward orientation has become the norm rather than the exception among developing nations. In fact, a remarkable convergence of views among academics and policymakers has developed on the virtues of what is variably called the Washington consensus, the market-oriented model, and the neoliberal approach.[1] Various advocates of delinkage from the world economy—nationalists, socialists, and "dependency" theorists—have now turned into ardent boosters of openness, a transformation that is perhaps nowhere more striking than in the person of Brazil's president, Fernando Henrique Cardoso, a former leading theorist of the dependency school.[2] As an Argentinean official has put it, "The old theme of the invading Yankee has given way to the wonderful Yankee driving the global train that you'd better board immediately or you're finished!" (quoted in Cohen 1998).

Tables 1.2 and 1.3 summarize the trends in tariff and nontariff barriers. As the tables show, Latin American countries in particular have drastically reduced their levels of trade protection since the early 1980s. Their average tariff and nontariff barriers are, with few exceptions, lower now than those that prevail in East Asia. Nontariff barriers have been reduced significantly in East Asia as well. However, Sub-Saharan Africa lags behind these two regions, especially with regard to the lowering of nontariff barriers.[3] Combine these developments with the dramatic opening of most of the former socialist countries of Eastern Europe and the post-Soviet states, and we have the widest-ranging trade liberalization the world has ever witnessed.

Judged by trade volumes, many developing nations are benefiting handsomely from an increasingly integrated world economy. According to the WTO, 11 developing countries were among the world's top 30 exporters in 1997 (Hong Kong, China, South Korea, Singapore, Taiwan, Mexico, Malaysia, Thailand, Saudi Arabia, Indonesia, and Brazil). If the European Union is treated as a single entity, eight more developing countries make the list (India, South Africa, United Arab Emirates, Turkey, Argentina, Philippines, Venezuela, and Israel). According to the Organisation for Economic Co-operation and Development (OECD), there are seven developing countries among the world's top 20 recipients of direct foreign investment (DFI): China, Mexico, Malaysia, Singapore, Argentina, Brazil, and Indonesia (OECD 1997). Many other developing countries, however, are falling behind,

TABLE 1.2. WEIGHTED AVERAGE TARIFFS BY REGION AND SECTOR
(percent)

Product Category	Primary Products	Food	Agricultural Raw Materials	Crude Fertilizers & Mineral Ores	Mineral Fuels	Nonferrous Metals	Manufactured Products	Chemicals	Iron & Steel	Machinery & Equipment	Other Manufactured Products	All Product Categories
Latin America & the Caribbean												
1980-83 (4-country avg.)	16.8	22.3	20.4	14.1	10.3	16.3	23.6	20.1	18.2	23.2	29.1	21.3
1984-87 (11-country avg.)	21.1	25.6	21.8	13.9	14.8	20.4	25.1	19.8	20.3	24.2	31.5	23.9
1988-90 (8-country avg.)	17.3	24.5	17.1	11.4	11.1	14.6	22.7	17.3	17.0	21.8	29.0	20.9
1991-93 (9-country avg.)	9.8	12.8	9.5	5.5	7.4	8.3	12.5	9.3	10.1	12.6	15.0	11.6
East Asia												
1980-83 (5-country avg.)	10.5	21.9	9.8	6.3	2.1	10.2	21.6	15.0	12.4	19.8	31.8	18.2
1984-87 (7-country avg.)	10.0	16.3	8.8	4.9	3.6	10.1	18.1	13.0	10.1	18.2	23.0	15.8
1988-90 (7-country avg.)	11.1	17.6	8.9	4.8	7.0	9.9	18.0	12.8	9.0	18.0	23.3	15.7
1991-93 (7-country avg.)	9.9	16.0	8.3	4.2	6.9	9.3	17.1	12.2	9.3	17.3	21.0	14.7
Sub-Saharan Africa												
1980-83 (13-country avg.)	24.4	33.8	24.4	17.9	14.3	21.5	32.8	23.5	19.6	31.8	43.6	30.2
1984-87 (13-country avg.)	20.1	25.4	20.0	14.7	13.7	18.5	23.5	17.7	19.0	22.7	30.1	22.6
1988-90 (10-country avg.)	18.9	30.6	15.4	10.1	8.1	14.5	22.5	14.8	14.8	20.1	33.3	21.3

Source: UNCTAD (1994).

Product Category	Primary Products	Food	Agricultural Raw Materials	Crude Fertilizers & Mineral Ores	Mineral Fuels	Nonferrous Metals	Manufactured Products	Chemicals	Iron & Steel	Machinery & Equipment	Other Manufactured Products	All Product Categories
Latin America & the Caribbean												
1984-87 (11-country avg.)	**42.8**	45.1	19.9	12.4	51.6	23.6	**28.4**	18.4	31.5	25.6	39.0	**32.9**
1988-90 (8-country avg.)	**48.6**	51.1	21.9	13.2	57.9	10.0	**20.9**	17.4	26.3	19.3	24.8	**30.3**
1991-93 (7-country avg.)	**16.1**	12.6	3.6	0.1	24.1	0.1	**1.8**	1.3	3.3	2.4	0.5	**6.6**
East Asia												
1984-87 (7-country avg.)	**31.1**	36.1	24.3	19.8	30.0	14.6	**23.1**	30.3	17.7	24.3	18.0	**25.6**
1988-90 (7-country avg.)	**18.8**	19.5	11.4	5.3	22.1	1.4	**8.3**	7.1	20.0	7.8	6.7	**11.8**
1991-93 (7-country avg.)	**11.2**	12.6	8.6	4.6	11.8	1.0	**5.5**	1.7	16.5	6.0	3.6	**7.4**
Sub-Saharan Africa												
1984-87 (13-country avg.)	**48.4**	61.7	43.0	32.6	45.5	39.3	**42.7**	28.7	48.3	41.1	52.4	**45.5**
1988-90 (10-country avg.)	**47.4**	58.6	45.9	38.0	39.1	46.7	**45.4**	40.5	47.3	43.5	51.4	**46.1**

Source: UNCTAD (1994).

particularly Sub-Saharan African countries, which have seen their share of world trade and investment flows shrink over the last three decades.

In the aftermath of the global economic turmoil that began in mid-1997, it is possible that many of these trends will be reversed. The financial panic that spread from Asia to Russia, and then on to Latin America, has altered the perceptions of many policymakers of the benefits of participation in the global economy. As these words were being written, in October 1998, Russia had defaulted on its obligations to foreign lenders, Malaysia had imposed strict capital and exchange controls, and even Hong Kong had undertaken some market-unfriendly measures in support of its stock market and currency. Normally restrained observers were suggesting that "global capitalism—whose triumph once seemed inevitable—is now in full retreat, perhaps for many years" (Samuelson 1998).

It is too early to judge how strong the backlash will be and how long it will last. Discontent so far has focused on the workings of the international financial system, and not on the trading regime per se. Russia aside, as of autumn 1998 no government was seriously contemplating restrictions on international trade or DFI. It is possible, and perhaps likely, that cooler heads will prevail and that an overreaction in the direction of protectionism and beggar-thy-neighbor policies will be avoided.

But preventing a backlash—today, or in the aftermath of the next crisis—also requires that we develop and promote a more nuanced, less ideological understanding of international economic integration. We need to be clearer about what the international economy can and cannot do for national economic development, about the complementary policies and institutions required domestically to sustain international economic integration, and about the fundamental determinants of successful national economic performance more broadly, without which an open world economy is not worth a dime. In other words, we need to know how to make openness work.

. . . .

MAKING OPENNESS WORK

■   AS I DISCUSS IN CHAPTER 2, OPENNESS CAN BE A SOURCE of many economic benefits. The importation of investment and intermediate goods that may not be available domestically at comparable cost, the transfer of ideas and technology from more developed nations, and access to foreign savings can help poor nations circumvent some of the traditional obstacles to rapid growth. The main theme of this book is that these are only *potential* benefits, to be realized in full only when the complementary policies and institutions are in place domestically. Furthermore, the gains that derive from openness have to be viewed in their proper perspective. The claims made by the boosters of international economic integration, I argue in Chapter 2, are frequently inflated or downright false. Countries that have done well in the postwar period are those that have been able to formulate a domestic investment strategy to kick-start growth and those that have had the appropriate institutions to handle external shocks, not those that have relied on reduced barriers to trade and capital flows. Policymakers therefore have to focus on the fundamentals of economic growth—investment, macroeconomic stability, human resources, and good governance—and not let international economic integration dominate their thinking on development.

Three propositions about openness constitute the starting point for my discussion in this book of economic policy in countries that are in the process of integrating themselves into the world economy.

First, openness by itself is not a reliable mechanism to generate sustained economic growth. The fundamental determinants of economic growth are the accumulation of physical and human capital and technological development. Openness can contribute to these determinants in ways that I discuss more fully in Chapter 2—by making cheap capital goods available for investment or by allowing the transmission of ideas from advanced countries, for example. But these potential linkages are contingent ones, requiring other pieces of the puzzle to fall into place. As I show, countries whose economies grow fast typically also become more open; but the converse progression—from increased openness to faster growth—is much less apparent.[4] I emphasize that this is not an argument against openness. It is a warning that a strategy of economic development that relies too much on encouraging exports and DFI, without emphasizing the complementary policies and institutions I discuss more extensively in subsequent chapters, risks disappointment and failure.

Second, openness will likely exert pressures that widen income and wealth disparities within countries.[5] The relationship between trade and wages has been discussed to date primarily in the context of the advanced industrial countries, with scholars trying to sort out the relative contributions of trade and technology to rising inequality. The evidence from the developing countries indicates that a similar rise in inequality has been experienced in many of the Latin American countries that have opened up their economies during the last two decades.[6] A striking example is Chile, which presents one of the most dramatic and successful cases of opening up. During the period of liberalization, the Gini coefficient[7] in Chile registered a 12-point increase (from 0.46 in 1971 to 0.58 in 1989), one of the largest jumps ever witnessed in any country over such a short period.[8] Of course, many other things happened in Chile during this period, including the repression of trade unions. But similar if less marked increases in inequality have been observed since the late 1980s in other economies choosing to open up rapidly, particularly in Latin America and among the formerly socialist economies.[9]

Hence, contrary to expectations, trade and investment liberalization appears to have increased the demand for skills in the developing countries, instead of reducing it. The beneficiaries, therefore, happen to be the better-paid, more highly skilled individuals. The reasons for this are not entirely clear. One possibility is that many of the activities that are complementary to exports and DFI—such as banking, finance, insurance, accounting, and other services—are quite intensive in the use of skilled workers.

Third, openness will leave countries vulnerable to external shocks that can trigger domestic conflicts and political upheavals. These consequences are damaging not only in their own right, but also serve to prolong and magnify the effects of external shocks. The developing world has been buffeted by a series of external shocks since the 1970s, arising from rapid changes in the terms of trade, spikes in world interest rates, and sudden reversals in capital flows. The protracted debt crisis of the 1980s in Latin America was a poignant demonstration of the consequences of the inability to handle external shocks. Shocks such as these will always be part of the global landscape. As the Asian financial crisis that began in 1997 demonstrates, no country, no matter what its trade orientation or the quality of its economic policies, is entirely immune to shocks. Therefore, the ability to manage turbulence in the world economy is a critical component of a strategy of making openness work.

Hence, openness is a mixed blessing, one that will need to be nurtured if it is to be a positive force for economic development. In the rest of this book, I discuss some of the complementary policies and institutions that are required. I emphasize the need for two strategies in particular: 1) a domestic investment strategy, and 2) a strategy of strengthening domestic institutions of conflict management. Introductory remarks about each follow.

The relationship between investment and growth tends to be erratic in the short run. Changes in investment do not have strong, determinate effects on growth rates over horizons of a few years or so (Easterly 1997). But in the long run, investment is key. Cross-national studies have shown that investment is one of the few robust correlates of economic growth over horizons spanning decades (Levin and Renelt 1992). The close association across countries between investment rates and economic growth since 1960 is depicted in Figure 1.1.

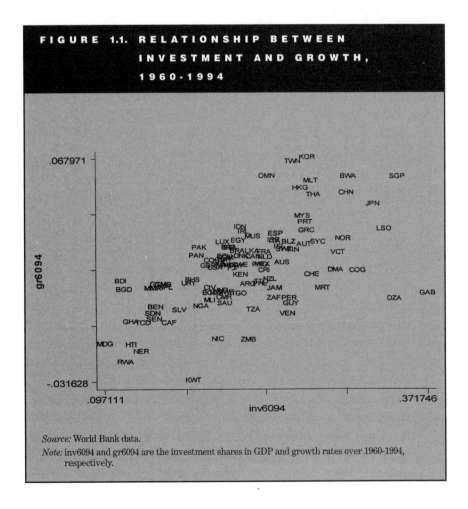

FIGURE 1.1. RELATIONSHIP BETWEEN INVESTMENT AND GROWTH, 1960-1994

Source: World Bank data.

Note: inv6094 and gr6094 are the investment shares in GDP and growth rates over 1960-1994, respectively.

Recent studies that have scrutinized the sources of East Asian growth have highlighted the overwhelming importance of accumulation for the countries in that region. In particular, these studies have found that total factor productivity (TFP) growth has played a minor role compared to physical investment (and increases in the quality and quantity of the labor force) in driving East Asian growth (Young 1995; Collins and Bosworth 1996). The proximate determinant of East Asia's performance has been its outstanding investment effort. South Korea, to take one of the most striking examples, was able to raise its investment rate from less than 10 percent of gross domestic product (GDP) in 1960 to 30 percent of GDP by the late 1970s.

Where has this investment come from? While opening up to the world economy can sometimes stimulate investment, it is a mistake to believe that there is a determinate relationship between openness and investment incentives. Standard economic theory suggests that the relationship between trade liberalization and the return to capital is generally ambiguous. If anything, in countries that are poorly endowed with physical capital, opening up would be expected to *reduce* the return to capital through Stolper-Samuelson channels, dampening private investment incentives.[10] As I discuss in Chapter 3, governments in East Asia complemented their outward orientation with a coherent domestic investment strategy that increased the private return to capital and kindled the animal spirits of entrepreneurs (see also Akyuz and Gore 1994). The South Korean, Taiwanese, and Singaporean governments went considerably beyond simply removing obstacles to private investment; they heavily subsidized it.

What drives economic growth in practice is a process whereby capacity expansion and the profitability of private investment feed on each other. There is no single way of raising the rate of private return to capital to start this process off. Even among South Korea, Taiwan, and Singapore, investment subsidies took different forms (see Chapter 3). Governments have to be imaginative in devising investment strategies that exploit their country's resources and capabilities, while respecting administrative and budgetary constraints. A useful starting point is to acknowledge that openness is *part* of a development strategy; it does not substitute for one.

Case studies of East Asian countries, as well as the systematic evidence from episodes of investment transitions (in Chapter 3), suggest that investment is causal where economic growth is concerned. An increase in investment, for whatever reason, tends to spur growth. However, one need not interpret the direction of causality too strictly. In practice, sustained periods of economic growth exhibit a symbiotic relationship between growth and investment, with each feeding on and in turn stimulating the other. As I show in subsequent chapters, such periods of takeoff can be ignited either by measures that encourage investment directly or by policies that create profitable production opportunities.

IMPORTANCE OF STRENGTHENING DOMESTIC INSTITUTIONS OF CONFLICT MANAGEMENT

As Figure 1.1 shows, the relationship between investment rates and growth across countries is a strong one, but it is not perfect. Over shorter time horizons, the relationship tends to disappear altogether. Most notably, only a small part of the decline in growth that many countries in Latin America and other regions experienced after the late 1970s is accounted for by the drop in their investment. As I argue in Chapter 4, the ability to maintain macroeconomic stability in the face of often-turbulent external conditions is the single most important factor accounting for the diversity of post-1975 economic performance in the developing world. The countries that were unable to adjust their macroeconomic policies to the shocks of the late 1970s and early 1980s ended up experiencing a dramatic collapse of productivity (which showed up in negative rates of TFP growth during the 1980s).

The countries that fell apart did so because their social and political institutions were inadequate to bring about the bargains required for macroeconomic adjustment—they were societies with weak *institutions of conflict management*. I use this terminology to indicate that adjusting to changing circumstances, and to external shocks in particular, requires the presence of institutions that can mediate distributional conflicts in society. In the absence of such institutions, the policy adjustments needed to reestablish macroeconomic balance are delayed, as labor, business, and other social groups block the implementation of fiscal and exchange-rate policies. The result is that the economy finds itself confronted with high inflation, a scarcity of foreign currency, and a myriad of other bottlenecks. Societies with deeper cleavages (along ethnic, income, or regional lines) are particularly susceptible to policy paralysis of this sort, making institutions of conflict management all the more important in such societies.

In Chapter 4, I illustrate and provide evidence for these ideas. I argue, on the basis of systematic evidence, that some of the more important institutions of conflict management are the following: participatory political institutions, civil and political liberties, free labor unions, noncorrupt bureaucracies, high-quality independent judiciaries, and mechanisms of social insurance such as social safety nets. These kinds of institutions are important both for managing turbulence in the world economy and for countering the potential widening of inequality that openness brings.

IMPLICATIONS FOR INTERNATIONAL GOVERNANCE

In this book, I focus mainly on the challenges faced by *national* policymakers. My primary concern is with domestic policies that foster national economic development, including those that complement openness to international trade and capital flows. Although my conclusions have implications for the governance of the international economy and the practices of multilateral organizations in particular, I do not develop these implications in detail. The question of how to reform international institutions so as to provide a supportive environment for the approaches outlined here is largely outside the scope of my analysis.

However, in the concluding chapter I briefly discuss a key lesson for international economic governance, which I repeat here: It is not realistic to expect that national development efforts will converge on a single model of "good economic behavior"; nor is it desirable that they do so. Correspondingly, the rules of the international economy must be flexible enough to allow individual developing countries to develop their own "styles" of capitalism, in the same way that countries such as Japan, Germany, and the United States have in the past evolved their own different models.

. . . .

CONCLUSION

■ DEVELOPMENT POLICY IS SUSCEPTIBLE TO FASHIONS. During the 1950s and 1960s, when import substitution was in vogue, there was excessive optimism about what government interventions could achieve (Krueger 1993, ch. 3). Now that outward orientation is the norm, there is excessive faith in what openness can accomplish. Early on, planning models emphasized capital accumulation at the expense of price incentives and the role of markets. Today, the importance of investment is consistently downplayed. The swing of the pendulum from one extreme to another creates blind spots, causing the risk of yet another unproductive change in fashion.

In reality, economies that have been successful have been those whose governments have done a whole host of things not only well but simultaneously. Successful economies have combined a certain degree of openness with policies that are conducive to investment, macroeconomic stability, and prudent management of capital inflows. Countries that have relied on any one of these alone typically have seen their national economies falter over the longer run. The policy lesson is a simple one, but it is often overlooked.

The arguments I make in this book have the implication that the terms around which openness is discussed in the developing countries need to change. The emphasis has to shift away from encouraging exports and DFI to thinking about how imports—particularly imports of ideas, of investment and intermediate goods, and of institutions—can enhance growth opportunities. Policymakers have to understand that integration into the world economy is unlikely to bring long-term growth on its own. They have to complement openness with other polices, including an explicit and coherent domestic investment strategy.[11] They have to realize that openness raises the premium on high-quality domestic institutions of conflict management, and that strengthening such institutions requires reforms that go beyond the standard economic remedies and adjustment packages.

Governments and policy advisers alike have to stop thinking of international economic integration as an end in itself.[12] Developing nations have to engage the world economy on their own terms, not on terms set by global markets or multilateral institutions. As I illustrate in subsequent chapters, successful economies in the past have been those that have taken a strategic and differentiated approach to openness. There is little reason to believe that the future will look any different.

NOTES

[1] The term *Washington consensus* was coined by John Williamson. For a useful collection of dissenting views on the new consensus, see Baker, Epstein, and Pollin (1998 forthcoming).

[2] "Leaping into the global economy is the only option," Cardoso is quoted as saying in the *Wall Street Journal* (December 15, 1995, p. A1). "If we don't do this, we don't have a way of

competing . . . It's not an imposition from outside. It's a necessity that we have." As *The New York Times* (November 20, 1994) put it on the occasion of Cardoso's election to the presidency, "If [he] had run for office in the United States, his opponent would have had a field day dredging up his past." (I am grateful to Avinash Dixit for the reference to *The New York Times* article.)

[3] The data for Africa are, as usual, patchy and not terribly recent. It is commonly accepted, however, that Africa's trade policies remain more restrictive than those in the rest of the world, despite a trend toward reform since the 1980s.

[4] This statement may appear to contradict a voluminous empirical literature on trade policy and growth. However, this literature has a number of conceptual and empirical flaws that render their interpretation problematic. For example, the indicators of trade policy that are employed often conflate tariff and nontariff barriers with macroeconomic imbalances (such as black-market premiums or real exchange-rate overvaluations). See Rodrik (1995c, section 4) for a discussion. Sachs and Warner (1995) have recently developed a measure of "openness" that is strongly correlated with growth and has received wide attention. This measure is a composite indicator that combines information on tariff and nontariff barriers with three other sorts of evidence: black-market premiums (an indicator of macroceconomic imbalance); a dummy for countries with export marketing boards (which is highly correlated with location in Sub-Saharan Africa); and a dummy for socialist countries (which is a broad indicator of political regime type). Very little of the action in this indicator is in the trade policy variables proper (i.e., tariff and nontariff barriers). On the one hand, excluding the information on tariff and nontariff barriers from the construction of the Sachs-Warner index yields regression results that are virtually identical to the original ones. On the other hand, a Sachs-Warner-like index that uses information *only* on tariff and notariff barriers does not enter the regression with a statistically significant coefficient. In other words, the strong empirical results that Sachs and Warner obtain derive from indicators other than trade policies.

[5] The ways in which international economic integration exacerbates domestic cleavages along lines of skills, mobility, and values is discussed in Rodrik (1997b).

[6] See Wood (1997) for a review of the evidence, and Feenstra and Hanson (1996), Pissarides (1997), and Wood (1997) for possible explanations.

[7] The Gini coefficient is a measure of income inequality. It goes from a zero for perfect equality, in which each person has the same income, to one for maximum inequality, in which one individual has all the income.

[8] The figures are from the Deininger and Squire (1996) compendium of income distribution data. The two figures are not strictly comparable, however, as the first is based on household incomes and the second on personal incomes.

[9] For the evidence, see Lora and Londono (1998, Figure 8) on Latin America and Kolodko (1998) on transition economies.

[10] According to the Stolper-Samuelson theorem, the removal of trade restrictions increases the real return to a country's relatively abundant factor of production and reduces the real return to the scarce factor. Note that the distributional evidence from Latin America discussed earlier contradicts the expectations derived from the theorem. Consequently, the theorem should not be taken very seriously in the predictive sense.

[11] For a recent and forceful statement on the need to complement trade liberalization and privatization with other reforms, see Stiglitz (1998).

[12] A good example of putting the trade cart before the development horse is the following recommendation from the OECD (1997, 18): "Though the speed and sequencing of liberalization will have to be determined by each country in light of its particular circumstances, policies should be geared to the *ultimate objective* of full integration into the global financial system" [emphasis added]. Note the grudging concession to "speed and sequencing."

Chapter 2
Openness in Perspective

WHY IS OPENNESS IMPORTANT?

■   THE ANSWER TO THE QUESTION POSED BY THIS SECTION'S TITLE may seem evident. Ask policymakers in Latin America, East Asia, or Eastern Europe about their reasons for opening up their national economies, and you will hear a long list of benefits. Most likely, these benefits will revolve around the importance of exports and DFI. Hence, you might be told that exports and DFI generate growth, that they create employment, that they produce learning spillovers that enhance the productivity of the economy, and that no country can afford to remain closed in a "globalized" world economy.

In fact, these are the wrong reasons for maintaining an open economy. The benefits of openness lie on the import side, rather than the export side. In general, there is little reason to believe that one dollar of exports will contribute to an economy more than a dollar of any other kind of activity, nor to believe that one dollar of DFI will contribute more than a dollar of any other kind of investment. As I discuss below, the evidence that exports and DFI per se generate economic growth, or that they produce significant positive spillovers, is scanty. Furthermore, the belief that exports can increase the overall level of employment in an economy over the longer term is a mercantilist fallacy, which, taken to its logical conclusion, leads to a preference for trade surpluses.

The starting point for any serious discussion of trade is the theory of comparative advantage. According to this theory, trade allows a more efficient use of an economy's resources by enabling imports of goods and services that could otherwise only be produced at home at higher resource costs. In particular, trade enables developing countries to import capital and intermediate goods—critical to long-run economic growth—that would be quite expensive to produce locally. As the theory emphasizes, exports are important only insofar as they allow imports to be paid for. Exports are the "price" an economy pays for having access to imports; they are a means, not an end.

More recent theories of "endogenous growth," going beyond models of static comparative advantage, have substantially enriched understanding of the channels through which trade can affect dynamic performance. These theories significantly widen the range of possibilities, but they do not create a presumption that openness spurs technological capabilities and long-run growth. On the plus side, the new models demonstrate how the benefits of scale that economies reap through participation in world markets and imports of technology can cumulate into faster growth over the longer term. On the minus side, these models underscore the risk of specialization in technologically less dynamic sectors—sectors in which developing countries might have an initial comparative advantage (see Grossman and Helpman 1991, ch. 9; Feenstra 1990; and Matsuyama 1992).

These are points that are well understood by economists, and they are not controversial. In their role as policy advocates, however, many economists have been too quick to latch on to protrade arguments that are weakly based on theory and ill supported by evidence. Just as the advantages of import-substitution policies were overstated in an earlier era, today the benefits of openness are oversold routinely in the policy-relevant literature and in the publications of the World Bank and the IMF. This is counterproductive both because it induces over-reliance on trade policy in national strategies for economic development, and because it increases the risk of a backlash against openness on the part of policymakers (and their constituencies) when the touted benefits fail to materialize.

Hence, it is important to be clear about what openness can and cannot do. Policymakers need to focus on the real benefits, and not get distracted by the more elusive and hypothetical gains. I emphasize four types of "imports" that openness enables countries to purchase: ideas, goods and services, capital, and institutions.

IMPORTING IDEAS

Ideas on organizing the process of production, manufacturing a new product, and (perhaps most fundamentally) identifying a commodity for which there exists a latent demand are central to economic growth. As Paul Romer (1993) has usefully emphasized, discussions of growth tend to focus on "objects" at the expense of the role played by "ideas." One advantage of backwardness is that ideas can be borrowed (i.e., imported) from richer countries: the wheel does not have to be reinvented in every country. Hence, the ability to import ideas is of particular advantage to countries that lag behind the technological frontier.

In his magisterial survey of world economic history, David Landes (1998) has argued that openness to ideas originating from abroad is a key distinction between "cultures" that have prospered materially (such as those in Western Europe) and those that have not. Importing ideas is different from importing goods. One can imagine countries that import high levels of consumer goods, yet fail to adopt and adapt the techniques developed by their trade partners—which is, in fact, how Landes interprets Chinese and Middle Eastern economic history. Conversely, South Korea and Taiwan have been very successful at importing ideas despite wide-ranging trade restrictions throughout the 1960s and 1970s. Successful importation of ideas requires individual skills and organizational capacity in the importing countries.

Romer (1993) distinguishes between strategies of "using ideas" and of "producing ideas." He points to Taiwan as an example of a country whose government has been successful in stimulating the domestic production of ideas by relying on a judicious mix of bureaucratic interventions and international trade. He compares this case favorably to that of Mauritius, where the government has instead relied on investments by multinational enterprises in an export-processing zone—a strategy of "using ideas." The first strategy produces greater economic rewards, but, as Romer emphasizes, it is also riskier because of the dangers of rent seeking and protectionism.

IMPORTING GOODS AND SERVICES

The traditional case for the gains from trade is based on comparative advantage: countries can increase their levels of well-being by importing those goods and services they produce relatively inefficiently and exporting those they produce relatively efficiently. Although the logical case for gains from trade is airtight, it is important to view these gains in their proper perspective. First, as stated, the traditional gains are of the static variety; that is, they raise the *level* of income, but not its long-run *rate of growth*. Second, under the standard perfectly competitive/constant-returns-to-scale scenario, the quantitative magnitude of the gains tends to be small—no more than a couple of percentage points of income in most cases.

More recent theoretical models of trade under conditions of imperfect competition or increasing returns to scale generate a much wider range of outcomes, as mentioned above. In particular, opening up to trade can result in increased rates of economic growth in so-called endogenous growth models. In the policy literature, this possibility is often used as an argument for a trade-growth linkage. What is less widely appreciated, however, is that endogenous growth models can also yield *permanently* reduced rates of growth, as when trade pushes an economy to specialize in sectors with no dynamic scale or other benefits. The theoretical relationship between trade and growth is fundamentally ambiguous.

In practice, there are two channels through which trade openness can have a significant positive effect on long-term economic performance in developing countries, one having to do with capital goods imports and the other with intermediate goods imports. A few words about each will clarify the argument.

IMPORTS OF INVESTMENT GOODS. For most developing countries, raising the long-term growth rate requires an increase in the investment rate. Cross-national evidence indicates that the social returns to equipment investment are particularly high: well over 50 percent, according to one careful study (Temple 1998; see also de Long and Summers 1991). Because developing countries lack a comparative advantage in producing capital goods, trade restrictions in such industries tend to be detrimental to growth. Trade protection raises the relative price of capital goods and reduces the level of *real* investment that is attainable for any level of savings.[1]

To take a numerical example, consider two countries with identical total savings rates (domestic plus foreign) of 15 percent of national income. Suppose country A imposes no import restrictions on capital goods, while B does, so that the domestic price of capital goods exceeds world prices by 20 percent in country B. In real terms, the investment that country B can undertake amounts to only 12.5 percent of its income (0.15/1.20), compared to 15 percent in country A. Indeed, countries where the relative price of investment goods has been kept high by trade restrictions and other policies tend to have lower investment rates, when investment and output are measured at international prices (see Figure 2.1). A 10 percent increase in the price of investment goods is associated with a one percentage point reduction in the real investment share in GDP. Therefore, countries that close themselves off from imports of capital equipment shoot themselves in the foot. In the postwar period, many Latin American and African countries fell into this trap. The paradigmatic case is Argentina, where capital equipment cost two to three times more than it did in the United States (see Taylor 1996, 1997).

IMPORTS OF INTERMEDIATE GOODS. The relationship between intermediate goods imports and economic growth is less direct but potentially as important. In any modern economy, production of manufactured goods relies on a large range of specialized inputs, many of which exhibit increasing returns to scale and require a high level of technological expertise. Developing countries, especially those with small domestic markets, cannot rely on a local supply of most of these specialized intermediate inputs. Trade impediments, which restrict the availability of such inputs, have adverse effects on the productivity of domestic manufacturing firms, and these cascade through the economy.

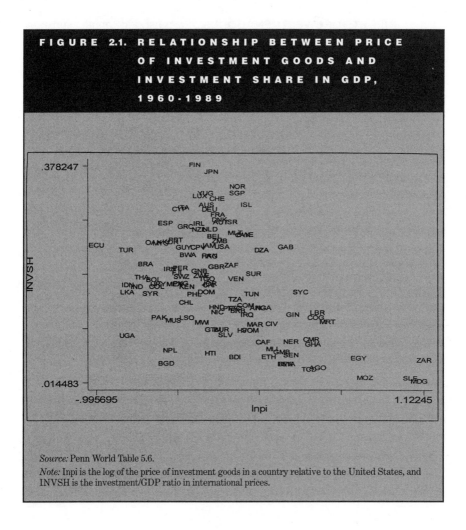

FIGURE 2.1. RELATIONSHIP BETWEEN PRICE OF INVESTMENT GOODS AND INVESTMENT SHARE IN GDP, 1960-1989

Source: Penn World Table 5.6.

Note: Inpi is the log of the price of investment goods in a country relative to the United States, and INVSH is the investment/GDP ratio in international prices.

Standard economic analysis focuses on the effect of trade restrictions on the level of *existing* activities. Romer (1994) has argued that one of the most important ways in which trade policy affects welfare in developing countries is by preventing the establishment of *new* activities. In the presence of fixed setup costs, new activities entail the loss of potentially large rectangles of consumer or producer surplus, rather than the relatively small Harberger's triangles of conventional analysis. Trade restrictions that make it not worthwhile for individual entrepreneurs to import key inputs and components—with the result that these become unavailable to the home economy—can have welfare costs that are several times larger than the costs suggested by the standard partial equilibrium.

IMPORTING CAPITAL

In principle, the ability to borrow from (and sometimes lend to) international capital markets is an important source of gain for developing countries. Almost by definition, developing countries are capital poor. All else being the same, this implies a rate of return to capital that is higher than elsewhere. A flow of capital into developing countries can therefore foster investment and growth. Second, borrowing allows the smoothing of consumption in response to the temporary shocks that often buffet poor economies—such as crop failures, natural disasters, or temporary terms-of-trade declines. Third, international capital markets allow households to diversify their portfolios and achieve a better mix of risk and return.

In practice, foreign borrowing has often been a mixed blessing at best. For one thing, there is little evidence that capital inflows crowd in additional domestic investments. In fact, the cross-national evidence indicates that a large portion of capital inflows substitutes for investments that would otherwise be financed domestically (see Bosworth and Collins 1998). Moreover, partly because of mismanagement on the part of heavily indebted governments and partly because of the herd instinct that dominates lenders' behavior, periods of sustained foreign borrowing frequently have ended in financial crises. The debt crisis of 1982, the Mexican peso crisis of 1994, and the Asian financial crisis of 1997 are the most recent examples of such episodes.

These experiences illustrate the difference in the way markets for financial assets operate. Although markets for goods and services are rarely textbook perfect, they do operate in most instances with a certain degree of efficiency and predictability. In financial markets, market failures arising from asymmetric information, incompleteness of contingent markets, bounded rationality, and occasional *ir*rationality are endemic. The consequences have been highlighted in the academic literature:

- Asymmetric information combined with implicit insurance results in moral hazard, adverse selection, and excessive lending for risky projects.

- A mismatch between short-term liabilities and long-term assets leaves financial intermediaries vulnerable to bank runs and financial panic, a problem that is particularly severe in cross-border transactions where there is no international lender of last resort.

- When markets cannot directly gauge the ability of the performance of money managers, these managers are likely to place too little weight on their private information and exhibit herd behavior, with the result being excessive volatility and contagion effects.

- Because asset values are determined by expectations about future returns, the dynamics of asset prices can be quite rich, exhibiting bubbles and "peso problems."[2]

Such problems are particularly severe where short-term capital flows—of maturity of less than a year—are concerned. Failure to roll over short-term debts in case of financial panic becomes more likely, and generates much more pain, in a country that has relied excessively on short-term flows. Compare, for example, two countries with debt-GDP ratios of 40 percent. Let short-term debt make up 80 percent of the first country's liabilities, and 20 percent of the second country's. In case foreign creditors refuse to roll over the debt, the first country has to turn over 36 percent of its GDP to its foreign creditors in one year, a burden that few countries would be able to shoulder. The second country has to transfer eight percent of its GDP, a significant but manageable amount.

The lesson is that reliance on DFI and long-term bond finance is comparatively much safer. Openness to international capital flows can be especially dangerous if the appropriate controls, regulatory apparatus, and macroeconomic framework are not in place. But even with such safeguards, short-term flows can prove erratic and risky.

International trade in goods, services, and capital entails arbitrage in prices: price differentials across national markets erode as a consequence of international integration. But international trade often entails another kind of arbitrage as well: arbitrage among national institutions. This kind of arbitrage is more subtle, and for that reason less discussed, but it is no less real.

Sometimes the arbitrage—institutional convergence—is the outcome of deliberate policy actions to "harmonize" a country's economic and social institutions with those of its trade partners.[3] Membership in the WTO, for example, requires the adoption of a certain set of institutional norms: nondiscrimination in trade and industrial policies, transparency in the publication of trade rules, and WTO-consistent patent and copyright protection, among others. Similarly, membership in the European Union (EU) requires the adoption of wide-ranging legal and bureaucratic requirements set down in Brussels. At other times, institutional arbitrage is the result of the working out of market forces. Mobility of employers around the world, for example, makes it harder to tax corporations and tilts national regimes toward the taxation of "nontraded" goods and factors (such as labor). Financial integration raises the premium for macroeconomic stability and makes central bank independence look more desirable. Finally, openness can change national institutions by altering the preferences that underlie them. Civil liberties and political freedoms are among the most important imported concepts in the developing world; the demands for democracy to which these ideas give rise are a direct product of openness in this broad sense.

Arbitrage in markets for goods and capital, in the absence of second-best complications, is associated with normatively desirable outcomes; as such, arbitrage increases efficiency. One cannot make the same presumption where arbitrage in institutions is concerned. There are no theorems that state that institutional convergence, harmonization, or "deep integration" (à la Lawrence 1996) through trade is inherently desirable. While many of the examples cited above involve outcomes that are desirable (greater democracy, for instance), not all possible outcomes are. Think of countries that face the prospect of adopting the EU's Common Agricultural Policy or its antidumping regime. It all depends on the circumstances and how national governments are able use such circumstances.

One way that governments can employ institutional arbitrage to good effect is by using it to enhance the credibility of domestic institutions. For example, the new disciplines imposed on developing country governments by the WTO—in the areas of tariff bindings, quantitative restrictions, services, subsidies, trade-related investment measures (TRIMs), and intellectual property—can be viewed as helping these governments to overcome traditional weaknesses in their style of governance. These disciplines impose a certain degree of predictability, transparency, rule-bound behavior, and nondiscrimination in areas of policy often subject to discretion and rent seeking (Rodrik 1995a). In the same vein, perhaps the greatest contribution of the North American Free Trade Agreement (NAFTA) to the Mexican economy was the element of irreversibility and "cementing" that NAFTA has contributed to the country's economic reforms. In Europe, the accession of Greece, Spain, and Portugal to the EU has made a return to military dictatorship virtually unthinkable.

However, imported institutions can also turn out to be ill suited or counterproductive. Many of the labor standards that some labor groups in the Northern Hemisphere would like developing countries to adopt—such as higher minimum wages or restrictions on some kinds of child labor—possibly fit into this category. The new patent restrictions called for in the IPR (international property rights) agreement of the WTO are at best a mixed blessing for countries such as India, for example, which have so far benefited from the domestic manufacture of cheap pharmaceuticals. A similar argument can be made about the tightening of environmental standards in developing countries. There are drawbacks, therefore, in harmonizing developing country institutions with those in more advanced countries.

. . . .

EXPORT FALLACIES

■ IF IMPORTS ARE IMPORTANT TO ECONOMIC DEVELOPMENT, so are exports, given that exports help pay for imports. In fact, this is exactly the right way to think of exports: they are a means, not an end. Because much of current thinking on trade policy in developing countries (and elsewhere) puts the cart before the horse by vastly overstating the role of exports, it is useful to elaborate a bit on this point.

Few countries' national economies have grown quickly over the last two decades without experiencing an increase in the share of domestic output that is exported. Table 2.1 lists the 25 fastest-growing developing countries over the 1975-1994 period, excluding those for which constant-price export data are unavailable. Only two countries among the 25 experienced declines in export-GDP ratios at constant prices (Indonesia and Egypt), with many of the rest showing spectacular increases of 10 percentage points or more. In this sense, increased export orientation has been a hallmark of practically all successful countries.

It is tempting to conclude from this kind of evidence that exports generally lead to or stimulate growth. Yet, as the next table shows, this would be an erroneous inference. In Table 2.2, I have reversed the exercise and listed the 25 developing countries with the largest increases in export-GDP ratios over the same period. The list includes many from the previous table (including most notably the East Asian countries), but also many with undistinguished growth records. For example, suppose we take one percent growth in GDP per capita (per annum) as the criterion for modest success. Close to half (11) of the countries in Table 2.2 fall *below* this threshold, with five having experienced *negative* growth. The evidence is clear: although countries that grow fast tend to experience rising export-GDP ratios, the reverse is not true in general.

The current emphasis on exports is in part a reaction to the neglect with which exports were treated under policies of import substitution. In the presence of high trade barriers, there is reason to believe that import levels are suboptimal, and that the economywide benefit from an additional dollar of exports exceeds a dollar because greater exports would enable a larger volume of imports. But with the worst trade restrictions gone in most countries outside of Sub-Saharan Africa, the efficiency case for favoring exports over other activities has disappeared as well.[4]

The intellectual case for exports nowadays revolves around the belief that exports provide a range of positive spillovers to domestic activities. Exports, it is claimed, are a source of learning and technological externalities for the home economy and allow domestic producers to learn from sophisticated markets abroad. Such statements are commonplace in World Bank reports, for example, where they are typically asserted without much substantiation (see World Bank 1993, ch. 6, and 1998, ch. 2).

TABLE 2.1. EXPORT-GDP RATIOS IN FASTEST GROWING COUNTRIES, 1975-1994 (at 1987 constant prices)

| | Per Capita GDP Growth 1975-1994 (percent) | Export-GDP Ratio | | |
		1975	1994	Increase 1975-1994
China	7.33	0.087	0.176	0.089
Korea, Republic of	6.95	0.208	0.424	0.216
Taiwan, China	6.56	0.316	0.538	0.222
Cyprus	6.05	0.247	0.521	0.274
Thailand	5.88	0.166	0.431	0.266
Hong Kong	5.76	0.729	2.098	1.369
Indonesia	4.93	0.377	0.246	-0.131
Malaysia	4.43	0.456	0.911	0.455
Chile	3.60	0.194	0.380	0.185
Lesotho	3.46	0.119	0.173	0.053
Egypt, Arab Rep.	3.17	0.240	0.217	-0.023
Pakistan	2.75	0.102	0.169	0.067
India	2.52	0.058	0.083	0.025
Colombia	2.07	0.150	0.208	0.058
Morocco	2.03	0.212	0.259	0.047
Bangladesh	2.00	0.059	0.131	0.071
Tunisia	1.98	0.305	0.445	0.140
Israel	1.85	0.245	0.357	0.112
Paraguay	1.69	0.199	0.590	0.391
Turkey	1.55	0.075	0.221	0.146
Uruguay	1.54	0.150	0.297	0.147
Dominican Republic	1.24	0.284	0.422	0.138
Myanmar	1.21	0.024	0.051	0.027
Mexico	1.13	0.108	0.299	0.191
Ecuador	0.99	0.280	0.353	0.073

Source: World Bank data.

TABLE 2.2. COUNTRIES WITH LARGEST INCREASE IN EXPORT-GDP RATIOS, 1975-1994 (at 1987 constant prices)

| | Export-GDP Ratio | | | Per Capita GDP Growth 1975-1994 (percent) |
	1975	1994	increase 1975-1994	
Hong Kong	0.729	2.098	1.369	5.76
Trinidad and Tobago	0.226	0.723	0.498	-0.12
Malaysia	0.456	0.911	0.455	4.43
Paraguay	0.199	0.590	0.391	1.69
Gabon	0.359	0.670	0.311	-4.11
Cyprus	0.247	0.521	0.274	6.05
Thailand	0.166	0.431	0.266	5.88
Philippines	0.161	0.386	0.225	0.42
Taiwan, China	0.316	0.538	0.222	6.56
Korea, Republic of	0.208	0.424	0.216	6.95
Mexico	0.108	0.299	0.191	1.13
Chile	0.194	0.380	0.185	3.60
Costa Rica	0.267	0.447	0.180	0.95
Swaziland	0.582	0.761	0.179	0.17
Cameroon	0.108	0.284	0.176	-0.62
Côte d'Ivoire	0.219	0.395	0.176	-2.87
Congo	0.370	0.520	0.150	0.67
Uruguay	0.150	0.297	0.147	1.54
Turkey	0.075	0.221	0.146	1.55
Tunisia	0.305	0.445	0.140	1.98
Dominican Republic	0.284	0.422	0.138	1.24
Rwanda	0.050	0.181	0.131	-3.29
Papua New Guinea	0.375	0.494	0.118	0.89
Israel	0.245	0.357	0.112	1.85
Mali	0.087	0.181	0.094	0.19

Source: World Bank data.

What does the evidence show? Many studies find that exporting firms are indeed technologically more dynamic, tend to have larger plants that better utilize scale economies, employ a mix of better-skilled workers, and generally outperform nonexporting firms. But these findings can be read in two different ways, with divergent implications for policy. One way is to interpret the evidence as support for the hypothesis that exporting activities are special along the stated dimensions. This then might constitute grounds for instituting policies that favor exports over other activities.[5] Another way is to take the position that the firms that are successful for other reasons tend to self-select into exporting activities (since that is what comparative advantage itself would suggest). In the latter case, exports would not require special treatment. The typical approach to date has been to document that exporters (or export-oriented sectors) in developing countries are superior along some technological dimension—say, total factor productivity growth (TFP)—and then to jump to the first conclusion (i.e., that exporting activities are special).

The authors of a number of recent studies have been more careful and have tried to sort out causality from correlation. Their conclusions suggest that the self-selection scenario is the more common one. For example, Clerides, Lach, and Tybout (1998) look at data from Colombia, Mexico, and Morocco and find little evidence that efficiency benefits accrue from exporting activities per se. What seems to happen is that efficient producers are more likely to enter export markets. Aw, Chang, and Roberts (1998) analyze TFP growth in Taiwan and South Korea and its relation to exporting. They find little evidence that learning from exporting has occurred in these two countries, even though exporters on average are more productive than nonexporters. In particular, there is no evidence that firms with a continuous export record experience an increasing productivity advantage over firms that never export.

In a number of careful studies, Bernard and Jensen (1995, 1998) have reached similar conclusions for the United States: while exporting plants outperform nonexporting plants in terms of size, productivity, and growth, there is no evidence that exporting status per se is responsible for these outcomes. Good performance seems to determine exporting status. Causality goes from productivity to exports, and not vice versa. As Bernard and Jensen (1995, p. 111) summarize their findings: "Current exporters have been successful in the past—it is likely that success has helped them become exporters—but there is no guarantee that current exporters will continue to outperform other establishments in the future." But a study by Bigsten et al. (1998) using a sample of firms from four African countries (Cameroon, Kenya, Ghana, and Zimbabwe) finds that exports have a significant impact on subsequent performance on technical efficiency, even when past levels of efficiency are controlled for.

Note, moreover, that even the occasional studies that find a positive relationship between exporting history and subsequent productivity performance (such as Bigsten et al. 1998) say nothing at all about the presence of spillovers (or positive externalities) across firms. In the absence of such spillovers, there is no economic argument for government policies that favor export activities, the reason being that the productivity benefits from exporting would be fully internalized by the firms in question and automatically provide the needed inducement for exporting.

In any case, these findings are indicative but preliminary. Future studies are likely to uncover a richer set of interactions between exports and performance. In the meantime, policymakers are well advised to discount claims of special significance for exports. We have no evidence to believe that a dollar of exports contributes any more (or any less) to an economy than a dollar of any other kind of productive activity.

Much the same can be said about DFI. The attitude of many developing-country policymakers toward DFI has undergone a remarkable turnaround in the last couple of decades, even more so than in the case of exports.[6] Multinational enterprises used to be seen as the emblem of dependency; they have now become the saviors of development. Today's policy literature is filled with extravagant claims about positive spillovers from DFI. These spillovers include technology transfer, marketing channels, superior management, and labor training.[7] Once again, the hard evidence is sobering. Systematic plant-level studies from countries such as Morocco and Venezuela find little in the way of positive spillovers (see Harrison 1996). At the national level, the effect of DFI on economic growth tends to be weak, and disappears as more country characteristics are controlled for (Bosworth and Collins 1998). Much, if not most, of the correlation between the presence of DFI and superior performance seems to be driven by reverse causality: multinational enterprises tend to locate in the more productive and profitable economies (and niches thereof).

The rule of thumb for DFI, as with exports, should be this: Absent hard evidence to the contrary, one dollar of DFI is worth no more (and no less) than a dollar of any other kind of investment. One implication is that subsidies and tax credits that favor foreign over domestic investment need serious reconsideration. A particularly pernicious form of subsidy to DFI is the erection of trade barriers so as to guarantee the foreign investor a protected domestic market—a concession that foreign investors are often able to extract from governments that are too keen on DFI. Such schemes have to be viewed as value subtracting for the economy as a whole (as per Brecher and Diaz-Alejandro 1977), unless a strong case can be made for the presence of positive externalities deriving from the investment in question.

EXPORT PESSIMISM

One of the pieces of conventional wisdom that shaped postwar development thinking was that developing country exports, mostly products based on natural resources, were largely insensitive to price policies. This was part of the reason why governments in Latin America and elsewhere de-emphasized exports and followed inward-oriented policies. In reality, such fears have proved to be unfounded. Countries that made a concerted effort to enhance the profitability of exports—via exchange-rate depreciation, export subsidies, or duty-free treatment of inputs for export production—experienced dramatic export booms. The list includes not only the usual East and Southeast Asian suspects but also countries such as Brazil after the late 1960s, Mauritius since the early 1970s, Turkey after 1980, and Chile since the mid-1980s. Neither low elasticities nor Northern protectionism has proved a serious obstacle to developing country exports. Cross-national studies generally conclude that the real exchange rate (its level as well as its variability) is a particularly significant determinant of export performance in developing countries.[8]

However, policymakers in many low-income countries—particularly those in Sub-Saharan Africa—continue to have misgivings about their export prospects. I discuss the case of Africa in more detail in Chapter 5. In the paragraphs that follow, I use a couple of non-African cases to illustrate how export pessimism is often misplaced.

TWO UNLIKELY CASES OF EXPORT SUCCESS

THE CASE OF TAIWAN. In 1954, the economists T. C. Liu and S. C. Tsiang were invited by the Taiwanese government to provide advice on economic policy.[9] At that time, Taiwan had an overvalued exchange rate, high levels of trade restrictions, and negative real interest rates—a classic combination of import-substitution syndromes. Liu and Tsiang promptly recommended devaluation coupled with trade liberalization. Taiwanese government officials objected, in line with then-conventional wisdom, that such policies would prove futile where exports were concerned. Indeed, Taiwan had even less reason to expect an export response than most low-income countries today. In terms adjusted for purchasing power, Taiwan had a poorer economy in 1955 than most African countries have today. Two commodities (sugar and rice) accounted for almost 80 percent of the island's exports, and, moreover, both were under quantitative ceilings imposed by international agreements. Sugar exports were regulated by the international sugar agreement, and rice exports, which went exclusively to Japan, were fixed by negotiation between the two countries' governments. Where would exports come from?

Liu and Tsiang replied that "even if the traditional major exports were confronted with foreign demands of little elasticity, there must be hundreds of new products that could be produced with cheap labor supply and readily sold in [other] countries" (Tsiang 1984, p. 306). The two economists were right: from the late 1950s on, Taiwanese exports grew phenomenally, and by 1970, industrial products made up almost 80 percent of exports (up from 10 percent in 1955). As I discuss in Chapter 3, trade and exchange-rate policies were not the only thing that made this export "miracle" possible: the Taiwanese government also had a coherent investment strategy that spurred growth and diversified the economy. The moral of the story is that current export structure is a poor indicator of future export prospects, once antiexport bias is removed and the other fundamentals are in place.

Taiwan had some advantages. In particular, it had a relatively abundant labor force, quite well educated for a country at that level of development, and therefore an underlying comparative advantage in manufactured goods.

THE CASE OF CHILE. Chile provides a recent example of successful export performance and diversification based on natural resources. In 1970, copper accounted for 77 percent of Chilean exports. Since then, and especially since 1985, when the depreciation of the real exchange rate made exports more profitable, nontraditional exports have expanded greatly. While close to 90 percent of Chilean exports are based on natural resources, copper's share has declined to below 50 percent, and the most rapid increases have been generated in agricultural products (mainly fruit such as grapes and apples), forestry products (sawn wood and wood pulp), and fish. The share of exports in GDP has gone from 14 percent of GDP in 1970 to 29 percent in 1985 and 39 percent in 1995. This process of export growth and diversification was enabled not only by open trade policies and (after the mid-1980s) a competitive exchange rate, but also by sector-specific government policies that encouraged technology transfer and investment in nontraditional areas (see Meller 1995).

Export pessimism can be a self-fulfilling prophecy, when antiexport bias is removed half-heartedly and reforms lack credibility. But regardless of whether a country's comparative advantage lies in manufactures or natural resources, the evidence shows that exports are responsive to incentives and that they do take off under the correct circumstances. Export diversification often occurs in tandem with export expansion, but it typically also requires complementary investment policies.

. . . .

CONCLUSION

■ THE THINKING ON TRADE AMONG DEVELOPMENT SPECIALISTS has gone from one extreme to the other during the last four decades. The belief that trade volumes are inelastic and that the developing nations would face great difficulty in making inroads in world markets for nontraditional products was the conventional wisdom in the aftermath of the Second World War. Multinational enterprises were viewed as agents of exploitation. Nowadays, trade and foreign investment have become the miracle cure for all that ails poor countries.

The good news, as I have suggested in this chapter, is that the export pessimism of the past has proved to be unjustified. The bad news is that trade and foreign investment are not all that their boosters advertise. The instinctive tendency of many policymakers nowadays to place priority on exports (over other types of production) and DFI (over other forms of investment) needs to be seriously challenged. Policymakers should avoid becoming knee-jerk globalizers. As I argue in the next chapter, it is domestic investment that ultimately makes an economy grow, not the global economy.

NOTES

[1] Many developing countries try to offset these costs by granting import duty exemptions to imports of capital goods.

[2] The "peso problem" refers to a process whereby the price of an asset (e.g., a currency) appreciates in order to balance out the risk that there will be a discrete depreciation at some point in the future.

[3] This is called "deep integration" by Lawrence (1996), to distinguish it from the "shallow integration" that takes place with the elimination of barriers to trade at the border.

[4] Note that when capital good imports entail positive externalities, as I argue above, there might be a case for subsidizing them. This means that exports also might provide additional value to the economy *to the extent* that their receipts are used to purchase capital goods. But there is no guarantee that they would be. Export receipts can be spent on purchasing consumer goods or accumulating foreign assets.

[5] *Might*, because there are other issues that need to be resolved before an economic case for subsidizing exports can be made. In particular, one needs to identify a specific market failure. For example, technological dynamism per se does not call for intervention unless there are conventional externalities involved. Wage premiums do not call for intervention unless they entail rents over and above returns to skills.

[6] For a useful and insightful account of the relationship between multinational enterprises and host governments, see Vernon (1998). Vernon argues that there are increased troubles ahead in this relationship.

[7] For example, a box titled "Technological Spillovers in the Sewing Machine Industry in Taiwan (China)," in World Bank 1997a, ch. 2, relates the story of the establishment of the U.S. company Singer in Taiwan. Yet upon closer reading, the spillovers in question turn out to be conventional input-output linkages and labor training. No evidence is presented for the presence of nonpecuniary externalities.

[8] See Elbadawi (1998) for a recent careful study focusing on nontraditional exports. Interestingly, Elbadawi finds that imports of capital goods are also strongly associated with nontraditional export performance. I emphasize the link between investment and exports in the next chapter.

[9] This account is based on Tsiang (1984).

Chapter 3
Investment
Strategies

TWO COUNTRY VIGNETTES

■   CONSIDER HOW THE GROWTH PROSPECTS for two actual countries, which I will call countries A and B, were evaluated by outside observers early in these countries' development history.

Country A was widely viewed as an economic basket case during the 1950s. The economy had virtually no manufacturing capacity, the investment rate was below 10 percent of GDP, and foreign aid financed nearly 70 percent of imports. The economy suffered from inflation, large black-market premiums, and other symptoms of macroeconomic instability. There were no natural resources to speak of. Foreign advisers routinely judged the local labor force to be lazy and ill prepared for the rigors of industrial production. The bureaucracy was viewed as incompetent and corrupt, rife with rent-seeking behavior in the allocation of licenses and permits. Few observers thought that the economy would ever be able to reduce its dependence on foreign assistance, let alone grow at respectable rates.

Country B had a monocrop economy, heavily dependent on sugar exports, and was facing a population explosion. The country had no natural resources or industrial base, and, as an island economy located far from international shipping lanes, was geographically isolated. In 1961, a committee headed by a future Nobel Prize winner in economics reached deeply pessimistic conclusions about the future of the island. In its report, the committee warned that unless something was done about the rapid growth of the population and, concomitantly, the labor force, the country was headed for catastrophe. When the country became fully independent, in 1968, the economic problems it faced were compounded by deteriorating external terms of trade, ethnic strife and riots, labor strikes, and a serious political challenge being mounted by Marxist political groups.

The two countries are South Korea and Mauritius, and we now know that in fact both countries did quite well for themselves.[1] Per capita GDP has grown at an annual rate of 6.8 percent in South Korea since 1960 and 4.1 percent in Mauritius since 1968. Poverty has been substantially alleviated, and social and human indicators have improved tremendously. Despite the pessimistic prognosis early on, the two countries are among the success stories of economic development. They have left behind most of the countries that were judged in the 1950s and 1960s to have better economic prospects.

It is no secret that the opportunities offered by international trade have had much to do with the success of these two economies. South Korea has turned itself into an export powerhouse, having metamorphosed from an insignificant producer of simple labor-intensive products into a major exporter of semiconductors. Mauritius has a less distinguished trading record, but without the ability to export garments produced in its export-processing zone (EPZ), the island would surely be a lot poorer than it is currently. In both economies, the volume of exports has expanded faster than GDP—at 17.2 percent per annum in South Korea (since 1960) and 5.2 percent in Mauritius (since 1968).

Although trade was undeniably important, in neither case was superior economic performance the result of a simple opening up to trade and foreign investment. The principal element behind South Korea's success was the government's ability to engineer a significant increase in the private return to investment. In Mauritius, the key was the channeling of a temporary boom in sugar profits into domestic investment via the creation of an EPZ. Where trade liberalization is concerned, the path taken by the two countries differed substantially from the rapid, across-the-board liberalization undertaken more recently in Latin America and typically recommended by the World Bank and IMF. Both countries liberalized in a gradual and partial manner throughout the 1980s; furthermore, economic liberalization occurred in tandem with other policies that maintained high levels of investment while keeping the social peace.

. . . .

HETERODOX OPENING IN MAURITIUS

■   MAURITIUS OWES ITS SUCCESS TO AN IMPORTANT EXTENT to the creation in 1970 of an export-processing zone operating under free-trade principles. Enterprises operating within the EPZ—which actually encompasses no particular geographic area—were granted tariff-free access to imports of machinery and inputs, free repatriation of profits, a 10-year tax holiday (for foreign investors), and "an implicit assurance that labor unrest would be suppressed and wage increases would be moderate" (Romer 1993, p. 77). The EPZ enabled a boom in garment exports to European markets, to which Mauritians could export quota free. In 1971, there were a mere nine enterprises in the EPZ, employing 644 people. Five years later, there were 85 EPZ enterprises, employing 17,171 workers, and making up 13 percent of the island's exports (Wellisz and Saw 1993, p. 241). Yet Mauritius has combined this EPZ with a domestic sector that was highly protected until the mid-1980s. Gulhati (1990, Table 2.10) reports an average effective rate of protection for manufacturing in 1982 of 89 percent, with a range of -24 to 824 percent (see also Milner and McKay 1996, pp. 72-73).

These high levels of protection were the legacy of the policies of import-substituting industrialization (ISI) followed during the 1960s. Under the Development Certificates (DC) scheme, local industrialists had been provided with tax holidays and protection from imports via tariffs and quantitative restrictions. A range of industries were set up using these incentives. The industrialist class that was thereby created was naturally opposed to the opening up of the trade regime.

The EPZ scheme provided a neat way around this difficulty. Wellisz and Saw (1993) make the point nicely:

A completely outward reorientation was politically unfeasible in the 1970s . . . since protection was the key to the prosperity of the import-substituting industry and DC certificate holders constituted a powerful lobby. But the DC certificate holders were not disturbed by the formation of an export-oriented enclave: on the contrary, they welcomed it as another potential source of profits. Mauritian labor also favored economic segmentation: the high-wage sector—sugar and import-substituting industries—constituted a male enclave. The EPZ industries employed women, whose earnings supplemented family incomes and who did not compete with the men. For the export-oriented industries, too, the enclave solution had obvious advantages in that the quasi-extraterritorial status provided a degree of protection against the government's dirigiste tendencies. (p. 242)

This passage illustrates the political advantages of the two-track strategy. The creation of the EPZ generated new opportunities for trade and employment (for women), without taking protection away from the import-substituting groups and from privileged male workers. The segmentation of labor markets was particularly crucial, as it prevented the expansion of the EPZ from driving wages up in the rest of the economy, and thereby disadvantaging import-substituting industries.[2] New profit opportunities were created at the margin while old opportunities were left undisturbed. There were no identifiable losers.

A crucial part of the story is that the EPZ export boom was predicated on a substantial investment in manufacturing capacity during the early 1970s, without which there would have been little garment production to export. The economy's investment rate rose from below 15 percent in the late 1960s to 30 percent a decade later. Where did this investment come from?

It did not come from abroad. In this respect, the experience of Mauritius is quite different from that of Singapore, which has relied heavily on foreign investment. In the early stages of the Mauritian EPZ, investments were financed virtually exclusively by *domestic* savings. This is shown clearly in Figure 3.1, which displays the domestic investment and savings rates for the Mauritian economy. The increase in investment in the early 1970s was more than matched by the increase in domestic savings. In fact, Mauritius did not rely on net foreign savings to any significant extent until 1976, well after the EPZ boom was under way. As late as 1984, only

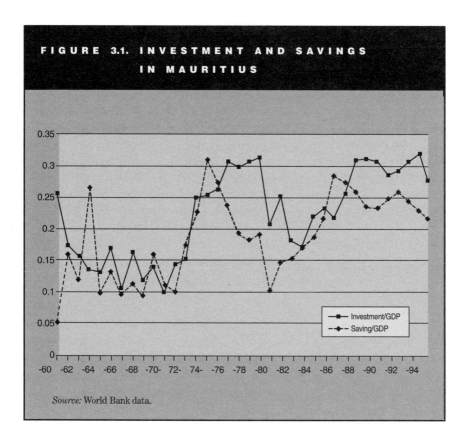

FIGURE 3.1. INVESTMENT AND SAVINGS IN MAURITIUS

Source: World Bank data.

57 percent of the capital stock was owned by foreigners, a far lower share than is usual for EPZs around the world (Hein 1989).

The increase in domestic savings was in turn the result of a fortuitous improvement in the island's terms of trade. World sugar prices began to rise in 1971, and the prices received by sugar producers more than tripled between 1972 and 1975 (Wellisz and Saw 1993, p. 235). By 1976 the trend was reversed, and domestic savings collapsed. But the spurt in the first half of the 1970s was critical in generating the funds that were then invested in the new export-oriented enterprises. The presence of strict foreign-exchange controls ensured that the savings would be invested domestically (Hein 1989).

The establishment of the EPZ just as sugar prices began their rise was a lucky coincidence that set the stage for an investment-export boom. Without the EPZ, there is a good chance that the investments would not have taken place, or else that they would have been wasted in high-cost, inward-looking projects. But without the increase in domestic savings and investment, the EPZ would not have been nearly as successful as it has been.

Although foreign investment did not play a major role in the early success of the EPZ, the expertise brought by the entrepreneurs from Hong Kong who established themselves in the Mauritian EPZ was arguably decisive. As Romer (1993) emphasizes:

> [the] entrepreneurs did bring a crucial array of ideas about the textile and garment business, including ideas on the specific kind of equipment to use, how to manage a small factory, how to manage relations with textile importers in the industrial countries, how to successfully exploit loopholes in quota limits, and hundreds of other ideas about running a modern garment assembly operation, such as knowledge of the sequence to use in sewing a shirt. (p. 78)

Hence, the EPZ constituted a politically astute strategy of partial opening up. It created a productive outlet for a domestic savings boom and enabled the importation of ideas about modern production and marketing.

. . . .

INVESTMENT POLICIES IN EAST ASIA[3]

■ IT IS NOW WELL RECOGNIZED that East Asia's phenomenal growth has been driven by physical investment. Table 3.1 shows a recent

TABLE 3.1. SOURCES OF GROWTH IN EAST ASIAN COUNTRIES, 1960-1994 (annual averages, percent)				
	Growth of Output per Worker	**Contribution of**		
		Physical Capital	**Education**	**Total Factor Productivity**
South Korea	5.7	3.3	0.8	1.5
Taiwan	5.8	3.1	0.6	2.0
Singapore	5.4	3.4	0.4	1.5

Source: Collins and Bosworth (1996).

disaggregation of the sources of growth for three East Asian countries, South Korea, Taiwan, and Singapore. In all three countries, the accumulation of physical capital is the most significant proximate determinant of growth. In South Korea, for example, 3.3 percentage points of the 5.7 percent growth in output per worker (or 58 percent) is accounted for by physical investment, with only 1.5 percentage points (26 percent) accounted for by TFP growth. Understanding East Asia's growth requires an understanding of the reasons for the investment boom.

EXPORT-LED GROWTH?

The standard story about East Asia is one of export-led growth. During the 1950s, the conventional account goes, South Korea and Taiwan engaged in traditional import-substitution policies, with multiple exchange rates, high levels of trade protection, and repressed financial markets. By the late 1950s, each country had exhausted the "easy stage" of import substitution. This, together with the impending reduction of U.S. aid—which had been the main source of foreign exchange for both economies—led policymakers in the two countries to alter their economic strategy and adopt export-oriented policies. These policies included the unification of exchange rates accompanied by devaluations, various other measures to stimulate exports (including, most significantly, duty-free access for exporters to imported inputs), higher interest rates, and some liberalization of the import regime. As a consequence of these measures, as well as a broadly supportive policy environment (encompassing macroeconomic stability and public investment in infrastructure and human capital), exports took off in the mid-1960s. Export orientation led both economies to specialize according to comparative advantage, with the results being rising levels of income, investment, savings, and productivity.

This orthodox account has been criticized for downplaying the active role taken by the Taiwanese and South Korean governments in shaping the allocation of resources. Observers such as Amsden (1989) and Wade (1990) have argued that the reforms of the 1960s went considerably beyond giving markets and comparative advantage free rein. According to these authors, governments in both countries had clear industrial priorities and did not hesitate to intervene (through subsidies, trade restrictions, administrative guidance, public enterprises, or credit allocation) to reshape comparative advantage in the desired direction. Interestingly, however, the orthodox and revisionist accounts converge on the importance of the export-oriented strategy in having disciplined firms and enhanced productivity growth. In its study, *The East Asian Miracle* (1993), the World Bank attempted to incorporate some of the revisionist objections (particularly on the role of directed credit) into the standard account.

Upon closer look, however, one discovers problems with the conventional story (Rodrik 1995b). First, the switch in relative incentives toward exports in the early 1960s was not significant enough to account for the export boom. Countries that have experienced sustained export growth outside of East Asia have almost always done so as a consequence of a sharp increase in the relative profitability of exports. What is striking about the experience of South Korea and Taiwan is how stable the relative price of their exportables was around the time of export takeoff. In both countries, most of the important export incentives had already been in place for several years before the export boom started. Once the boom got under way, it picked up speed even though the measured profitability of exports did not increase further. Moreover, exports continued their inexorable growth, often in the context of *deteriorating* incentives for exporting activities.[4]

Second, it is not clear why export orientation (or the increase in exports) should have led to an investment boom. There are many cases in which even more sizable increases in the profitability of exports have either not led to increases in investment or have done so only after a considerable lag. This is important insofar as exports (unlike investment) do not directly lead to economic growth.

Consider two important examples, Turkey and Chile. In Turkey, there was a massive increase in the profitability of exports in the early 1980s on the order of more than 50 percent, with considerable import liberalization as well. These reforms were accompanied by an impressive increase in the export-GDP ratio. Yet the level of private investment actually fell in this period and did not recover until the second half of the 1980s. In Chile, an investment boom accompanied a fall in the relative profitability of exports in the late 1970s. Investment eventually collapsed during 1982-83, as a result of a major financial crisis. Export incentives increased significantly after 1982, but private investment responded sluggishly until 1989.

It should not be surprising that export incentives and investment can covary in different ways. In theory, there is no reason to suppose that export orientation should be associated with an increase in investment demand. Export orientation makes some sectors more profitable and others (import-competing activities and nontradables) less so. The same is true of import liberalization. The net effect on investment demand is indeterminate. If anything, the logic of relative factor endowments and the Stolper-Samuelson theorem yields an opposing presumption: in capital-poor countries such as Taiwan and South Korea during the 1950s and 1960s, an increase in the relative price of exports should have been associated with a *decline* in the return to capital and hence reduced investment.

Third, because the export base in East Asia was typically quite small early on, the contribution of exports to GDP growth could not have been very high until at least the mid-1970s. In a fully employed, small open economy with marginal products of productive factors equalized among different activities, an increase in exports cannot, in any case, raise output. During much of the 1960s, South Korea and Taiwan had some unemployment, as well as a productivity gap between the modern and traditional sectors of their economies. Under such conditions, an increase in exports can be expansionary, but the question is by how much? Exports were less than five percent of GDP in South Korea around 1960, and barely over 10 percent in Taiwan. In a pure accounting sense, exports could not have been responsible for more than a small fraction of the initial growth spurt in both countries, in view of the small base that they constituted.

Fourth, it is not clear that export growth was, or should have been, associated with cumulative productivity spillovers to the rest of the economy.

There is a common presumption that the contribution of exports to growth came not from the demand side or through investment, but from widespread technological spillovers and cumulative productivity benefits deriving from export performance. The World Bank's 1993 East Asia report gives this explanation top billing in its exposition of the "dynamic" benefits of outward orientation. However, as I discussed in the previous chapter, there is virtually no credible evidence that exports or outward orientation were strongly associated with technological externalities.

In both South Korea and Taiwan, manufactured exports accounted for a quarter or less of total exports around 1960, and consequently they constituted a tiny share of national income. It is not easy to see how the spillovers from such a minuscule source, to the extent that they existed at all, could have been so strong as to set a process of aggregate economic growth into motion. Note, moreover, that overall productivity growth in manufacturing industry has not been spectacular in either country and can explain only a small part of total growth.

INVESTMENT INCENTIVES

SOUTH KOREA AND TAIWAN. One of the most important economic changes in the late 1950s in Taiwan and the early 1960s in South Korea was a transformation in government priorities. During much of the 1950s, economic goals had not ranked particularly high with either the Taiwanese or the South Korean leaderships. In Taiwan, the government was preoccupied with the reconquest of the Chinese mainland. In South Korea, President Syngman Rhee's attention was focused on national consolidation and other, narrower political goals. But by the end of the 1950s in Taiwan and the early 1960s in South Korea, economic growth became a top priority of the leadership in both countries.

In Taiwan, a turning point was the Nineteen-Point Reform Program instituted in 1960. This included a wide range of subsidies for investment and signaled a major shift in government attitudes toward investment. As Lin (1973, p. 96) has written, "[With] the announcement of the nineteen-point reform program of 1960, the improvement of investment climate became a catchword. The simplification of administrative procedures and the liberalization of regulative measures with regard to economic matters became an official goal." And in South Korea, President Chung Hee Park, who took power in a military coup in 1961, could not have been more different from his predecessor. Park gave precedence to economics over politics, and to economic growth over other economic concerns, which was reflected in the amount of time he spent supporting growth-oriented bureaucrats and businessmen (see Jones and Sakong 1980, pp. 40-43). Early in his rule, Park made very clear that entrepreneurs who undertook investments in line with his priorities would be richly rewarded (while others would be penalized). Hence, in both countries there was a sharp change in the investment climate.

In addition to eliminating obstacles to investment, government policy heavily subsidized investment. In South Korea, the chief form of investment subsidy was the extension of credit to large business groups at negative real interest rates. South Korean banks were nationalized after the coup of 1961, and consequently the government obtained exclusive control over the allocation of investable funds in the economy. According to Jones and Sakong (1980, p. 104), "the general bank [lending] rate has typically been half of the curb-market rate; and second, the real bank rate has often been negative and generally below even the most conservative estimates of the opportunity cost of capital." Another important manner in which investment was subsidized in South Korea was through the socialization of investment risk in selected sectors. This emerged because the government—most notably President Park himself—provided an implicit guarantee that the state would bail out entrepreneurs investing in "desirable" activities if circumstances later threatened the profitability of those investments.

In Taiwan, investment subsidies took different forms. Real lending rates were generally positive and credit subsidies were much less important. The most important direct subsidies in Taiwan came in the form of tax incentives. The Statute for Encouragement of Investment (enacted in 1960 in conjunction with the Nineteen-Point Reform Program) represented a "sweeping extension" (Lin 1973, p. 85) of the prevailing tax credit system for investment. The maximum business income tax paid by enterprises was reduced to 18 percent of annual income (from a previous maximum of 32.5 percent); the tax holiday for new investments was extended from three years to five years; tax exemption was given to undistributed dividends for reinvestment and the proceeds of export sales; in regard to the stamp and deed taxes on "productive" real estate, exemptions or taxation at reduced rates was granted; and payments of import duties on plant equipment were made deferrable, and payable in installments once operations commenced. These incentives were further expanded in 1965, at which time the business income tax was reduced in all priority sectors listed in the investment law, and specified manufacturing sectors (in basic metals, electrical machinery and electronics, machinery, transportation equipment, chemical fertilizers, petrochemicals, and natural-gas pipe) were given complete exemption from import duties on plant equipment.[5]

In addition to providing subsidies, the South Korean and Taiwanese governments played a much more direct, hands-on role by involving private entrepreneurs in investments they may not have otherwise made. In both cases, there are good case histories of how the government actively took steps to ensure that private entrepreneurs would invest in certain areas. In Taiwan, it was the government that took the initial steps in establishing such industries as plastics, textiles, fibers, steel, and electronics. In South Korea, as Amsden has written (1989, pp. 80-81), "the initiative to enter new manufacturing branches has come primarily from the public sphere. Ignoring the 1950s, . . . every major shift in industrial diversification in the decades of the 1960s and 1970s was instigated by the state."

Finally, public enterprises played a crucial role in enhancing the profitability of private investment in both countries (perhaps more so in Taiwan than in South Korea) by ensuring that key inputs were available locally for private producers downstream. In Taiwan, it was common for the state to establish new upstream industries and then either hand the factories over to selected private entrepreneurs (as in the case of glass, plastics, steel, and cement) or run them as public enterprises (Wade 1990, p. 78). In South Korea, the government established many new public enterprises in the 1960s and 1970s, particularly in basic industries characterized by a high level of linkages and scale economies (Jones and Sakong 1980). In both countries, public enterprises were the recipients of favorable credit terms, as well as direct allocations from the government budget. Not only did public enterprises account for a large share of manufacturing output and investment in each country, their importance actually increased during the critical takeoff years of the 1960s.

SINGAPORE. Investment was heavily subsidized in Singapore as well. The year 1968 marked a dramatic expansion of the Singaporean government's involvement in investment activities, with the Development Bank of Singapore increasing its financial commitments eightfold over a two-and-a-half year period (Young 1992, p. 21). A substantial share of the economy came to be owned, directly or indirectly, by the Singaporean government as a result. These huge investments were funded by surpluses on the current account of the government budget, as well as by borrowing from the Central Provident Fund (Young 1992).

Unlike South Korea and Taiwan, Singapore focused its incentives heavily on foreign investors. According to Young (1992), 1968 marked a turning point with regard to foreign investment as well. Labor legislation enacted that year significantly strengthened management's bargaining power over issues of pay, benefits, and other working conditions. A wide range of tax incentives for investors were phased in or expanded after 1967, with exemptions from taxes on profits taking the lead. Although in principle these incentives did not discriminate between domestic and foreign investors, "because they are usually linked to sizable investments involving advanced technologies in new (targeted) industries, the overwhelming majority of participants [were] foreign" (Young 1992, p. 23).

Young emphasizes that Singapore's Pioneer Industries Ordinance, the source of the most significant tax holidays provided to foreign investors, dates from 1959. He notes that the ordinance failed to attract much foreign investment "until after 1968, when the Singaporean government began to expand its own financial participation in manufacturing and other sectors" (1992, p. 24). He suggests that after that date the government subsidized foreign investment beyond the tax incentives themselves, at exorbitant rates.

DISCUSSION. In economies with complete markets, investment subsidies of the kind just discussed will reduce real income, even if they end up increasing investment. However, this hardly applies to Taiwan, South Korea, or Singapore in the 1960s. The more realistic presumption is that a range of market failures kept investment at a level below what would have been socially optimal. I have argued elsewhere (Rodrik 1996a) that there is a prima facie case for the existence of coordination failures in private-sector investment decisions during the early stages of development in economies such as that of South Korea, Taiwan, and Singapore. This accounts for why large-scale investments would turn out to be privately (and socially) profitable while individual investments were perceived as unprofitable in the absence of government inducements. One way of viewing investment subsidies in these economies, then, is as policies that alleviated such coordination failures.

In his well-known essay on Singapore and Hong Kong, on which I have drawn above, Alwyn Young (1992) argues that the Singaporean government's aggressive proinvestment policies were largely to blame for what, to Young, appear to be a poor aggregate TFP growth record in manufactures. In comparison, Hong Kong has been a paragon of free markets, with a much better productivity performance.[6]

At first blush, Hong Kong's experience would appear to confirm that it is primarily (if not exclusively) "fundamentals" that matter, with industrial policies that stimulate investment playing either no role or a negative one. Indeed, Hong Kong is the standard counterexample to analyses that posit a useful role for activist government policies. However, this is a misreading of the evidence. By 1960 Hong Kong was already a relatively wealthy country, with a high investment rate and favorable growth prospects. Unlike the other three East Asian countries, Hong Kong did not face a fundamental developmental challenge. There was much less need for an investment strategy.

Figure 3.2 shows investment rates for the four East Asian countries since the early 1960s. As the figure makes clear, Hong Kong was already a high-investment country by the mid-1960s, when the World Bank data start. In 1965, the first year for which the World Bank provides investment data for Hong Kong, the investment rate there was 38 percent, compared to 11 percent in South Korea, 23 percent in Singapore, and 12 percent in Taiwan (all at 1987 relative-prices). According to the Penn World Tables,[7] which do provide earlier figures for investment rates, the figure for 1960 is 24 percent for Hong Kong, compared to 7 percent for South Korea, 11 percent for Singapore, and 15 percent for Taiwan. Whichever source is used, it is clear that Hong Kong's investment rate was substantially higher by the early 1960s than that of any of the other countries.

For historical reasons having to do with its entrepôt role in international trade, Hong Kong was already a relatively rich country in 1960, with a per capita income of $2,222 (1985 U.S. dollars), a level that South Korea and Taiwan would not reach for at least another decade. Hong Kong's transition to high investment levels appears to have taken place largely during the 1950s, when the country was a haven of economic and political stability in the region. There were major inflows of capital from China and elsewhere. Hence, one can argue that Hong Kong did not face the central challenge of economic development—how to transform a low-saving, low-investment economy into a high-saving, high-investment one—in quite the same way that the other economies did.

Furthermore, Hong Kong is the only country in the region that has not experienced a steady and sustained increase in investment (as a share of GDP) since the early 1960s (see Figure 3.2). This is also consistent with the absence of an explicit investment strategy: the government's noninterventionist stance is reflected in a flat investment ratio. Arguably, this has not been costly insofar as the Hong Kong economy had already reached a certain degree of maturity. The other countries of the region started from considerably lower levels and needed their governments to give accumulation a push.

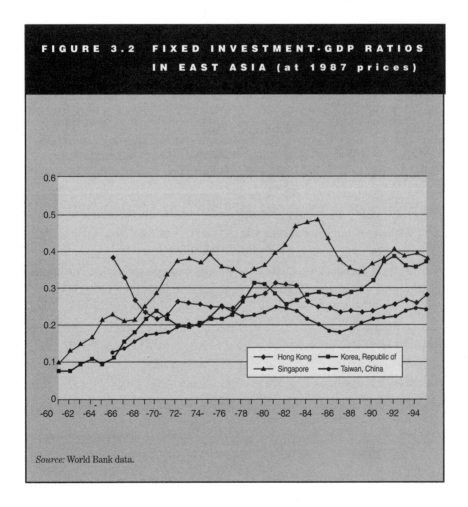

FIGURE 3.2   FIXED INVESTMENT-GDP RATIOS IN EAST ASIA (at 1987 prices)

Legend:
- Hong Kong
- Korea, Republic of
- Singapore
- Taiwan, China

Source: World Bank data.

Hong Kong's experience suggests that a hands-off attitude toward investment can be effective when the level of investment is already comparatively high and the appropriate institutions are in place. At the same time, far from suggesting the irrelevance of interventionist policies, Hong Kong's experience confirms that a sustained increase in the domestic investment effort is unlikely to be achieved in the absence of government policies directed toward that aim.

. . . .

INVESTMENT TRANSITIONS

■   COUNTRIES THAT ARE ABLE TO ENGINEER INCREASES in their investment efforts experience faster economic growth. They also become more outward oriented and witness a rising share of exports in GDP. Hence, investment transitions produce richer economies that are more integrated with the world economy.

These statements are patently true for the handful of countries whose experiences I have so far described. But are they true in general? Because an investment-centered approach to economic development raises eyebrows nowadays, it is important to get the stylized facts straight.

In this section, I take a broader cut at analyzing the contours of investment transitions and present the results of a statistical exercise covering all developing countries for which I have data. The purpose is to identify "episodes" of investment transitions and to delineate their consequences by comparing trends in economic growth and exports before and after such transitions. For the purposes of this exercise, I define an investment transition as a sustained increase in the investment/GDP ratio of five percentage points or more. Specifically, a country is said to undergo an investment transition at year T if the three-year moving average of its investment rate over an eight-year period starting at T+1 exceeds the five-year average of its investment rate prior to T by five percentage points or more. I exclude major oil-exporting countries and the developed countries. I also exclude cases in which the post-transition investment rate remains below 10 percent. To maximize the available sample size, I derive the investment rate from gross fixed capital investment as a share of GDP at current prices. All data come from the World Bank.

The exercise yields 47 episodes of investment transitions, listed in Table 3.2. The table shows the year of the transition for each country listed, as well as the investment rates before and after the transitions. The median investment rate for all the countries listed rises from 15 to 26 percent of GDP following the transition. The table includes the well-known cases I have already discussed: South Korea (1965), Singapore (1965), and Mauritius (1971).[8] Many of the other instances are also familiar: Botswana (1966), Chile (1986), China (1970), Indonesia (1969), and Thailand (1966). But there are others that would have easily escaped notice in the absence of a systematic search. The advantage of this approach is that we can make generalizations that go beyond the well-known, well-studied cases.

What happens to economic growth and exports following investment transitions? The simplest way to analyze the average tendencies in the data is to reorder the annual data for each country according to "transition years." Take, for example, the case of Botswana, with transition year 1966. If T = 1966, Botswana's growth rate for 1965 becomes its growth rate for T-1, its growth rate for 1967 becomes its growth rate for T+1, and so on. We then calculate the median values of the relevant indicator across countries for corresponding transition years. The trends in these median values can help us create a picture of the "typical" pattern.[9]

Figure 3.3 tells the story with respect to growth. It displays the median investment and growth rates for the sample of countries that have undergone investment transitions, with the country data ordered according to transition years as described above. The growth rates shown are relative to world averages, to eliminate the effect of global trends in growth, and they have been smoothed by taking a three-year moving average (centered on the year in question). As the figure shows, investment transitions are associated with significant increases in economic growth. The underlying data reveal that countries that experience an investment transition go from a growth rate which is 0.8 percentage points less than the world average to one that is 1.4 percentage more than the average (with each average calculated for the five years pre- and post-transition). This is a difference of 2.2 percentage points, which is quite significant.

The figure also reveals that some of the growth gains are eventually reversed, even though the level of investment remains high. This finding reflects the fact that many of the countries listed in Table 3.2 did a lousy job of handling the external shocks of the 1970s and later. I argue in the next chapter that this is the result of the poor quality of their institutions of

TABLE 3.2. COUNTRIES WITH INVESTMENT
TRANSITIONS

| Country | Transition year | Average investment/GDP ratios | |
		5 years prior	5 years after
Botswana	1966	0.119	0.348
Burkina Faso	1970	0.096	0.229
Burundi	1976	0.055	0.142
Cameroon	1976	0.184	0.273
Cape Verde	1978	0.315	0.561
Chile	1986	0.157	0.243
China	1970	0.219	0.289
Cyprus	1976	0.252	0.365
Egypt, Arab Rep.	1973	0.130	0.290
Gambia	1975	0.064	0.222
Guinea-Bissau	1978	0.178	0.256
Guyana	1973	0.209	0.293
Haiti	1970	0.070	0.145
Indonesia	1969	0.093	0.193
Jamaica	1981	0.161	0.220
Jordan	1973	0.183	0.324
Kenya	1966	0.140	0.216
Kiribati	1977	0.076	0.363
Korea, Republic of	1965	0.141	0.250
Lesotho	1971	0.109	0.213
Malawi	1965	0.098	0.182
Mauritania	1974	0.213	0.345
Mauritius	1971	0.126	0.245
Morocco	1969	0.113	0.178
Mozambique	1985	0.188	0.389
Nepal	1974	0.070	0.159
Nicaragua	1983	0.133	0.215
Niger	1972	0.084	0.156
Papua New Guinea	1965	0.150	0.273
Paraguay	1973	0.152	0.243
Philippines	1973	0.209	0.304
Sao Tome and Principe	1975	0.164	0.284
Singapore	1965	0.152	0.273
Somalia	1972	0.120	0.230
South Africa	1965	0.216	0.282
Sri Lanka	1978	0.151	0.294
Swaziland	1976	0.221	0.344
Syrian Arab Rep.	1972	0.136	0.259
Tanzania	1969	0.157	0.228
Thailand	1966	0.186	0.247
Togo	1971	0.137	0.223
Tunisia	1974	0.217	0.299
Uruguay	1971	0.128	0.231
Venezuela	1968	0.237	0.318
Yemen, former Arab Republic of	1975	0.176	0.355
Zambia	1965	0.206	0.293
Zimbabwe	1967	0.150	0.223

Source: World Bank data.

conflict management. We note for now that, even after this decline, growth performance remains superior when compared to pre-transition rates. The average growth rate in years [T+11, T+15] (once the change in world growth is taken out) is still 1.1 percentage points above the corresponding rate for years [T-5, T-1].

The results with respect to export performance are shown in Figure 3.4. The figure reveals a steady and unmistakable increase in export/GDP ratios following on the heels of investment transitions. Prior to the first year of the transition, exports are flat, with the median value slightly less than 20 percent of GDP. This number increases to 22 percent in years [T, T+4] and to 27 percent in years [T+5, T+9], stabilizing thereafter. The cumulative

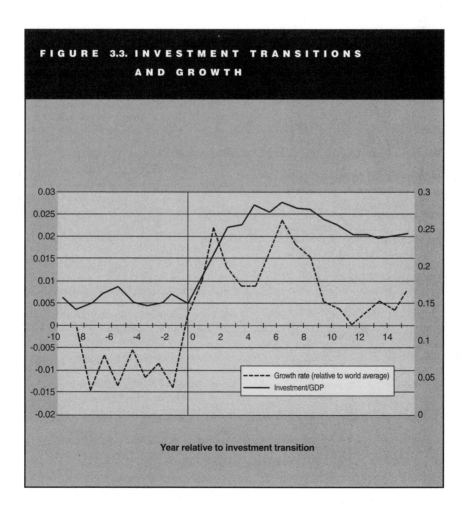

FIGURE 3.3. INVESTMENT TRANSITIONS AND GROWTH

Year relative to investment transition

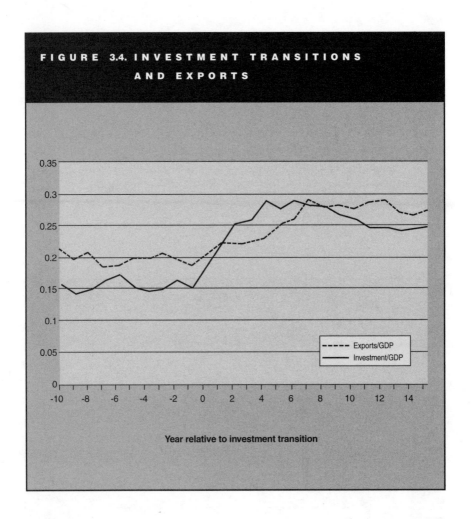

FIGURE 3.4. INVESTMENT TRANSITIONS
AND EXPORTS

0.35
0.3
0.25
0.2
0.15
0.1
0.05
0

-10   -8   -6   -4   -2   0   2   4   6   8   10   12   14

- - - - - Exports/GDP
——— Investment/GDP

Year relative to investment transition

effect of an investment transition is a rise in the export/GDP ratio of more than seven percentage points over a period of a decade. Hence, investment is good not only for growth, but for export performance as well.

. . . .

CONCLUSION

■   THE INTELLECTUAL CLIMATE REGARDING physical investment has changed radically since the heyday of "capital fundamentalism" in the 1950s, so much so that one can pick up comprehensive reports on economic prospects for developing countries and not encounter a single word about the importance of investment—except for foreign investment, of course, which is typically judged to be critically important (e.g., World Bank 1997a). Macroeconomic stability, free markets, and small government, it is asserted (or implied), are all that is necessary.

For countries with a well-established entrepreneurial class and an investment rate already at or above, say, 25 percent, this presumption may well be right. But for poorer countries with low levels of private investment and nondiversified production structures, more is likely to be needed. The lesson from East Asia is clear: the three East Asian "dragons" with low investment rates in the early 1960s—South Korea, Taiwan, and Singapore—would not have been nearly as successful had their governments not given capital accumulation a big push by subsidizing, cajoling, and otherwise stimulating private investors. The evidence from East Asia and elsewhere shows that investment booms produce economic growth as well as greater export orientation. The evidence also implies that low levels of saving per se are not a significant obstacle to growth: household and corporate saving rates typically rise as profitable investment opportunities are exploited.

There is no hard-and-fast rule about what kind of strategy will work best in producing these investment transitions. The range of policies that are pursued varies greatly even among the East Asian countries. For example, compare the emphasis on subsidizing foreign investment in Singapore with the discouragement of DFI in South Korea. A starting point is to remove policies—including trade restrictions—that keep the domestic price of investment goods high. Probably the most damaging aspect of trade restrictions in many Latin American and African countries has been their contribution to keeping the relative price of capital equipment high, and, therefore, investment rates low. Where investment subsidies are already in place, another important priority is to simplify the incentive regime so as to clarify objectives, provide transparent inducements, and reduce bureaucratic red tape.

Beyond these, much depends on the specific circumstances of the country and the imagination of policymakers. In general, smaller countries have fewer options and must bear in mind that policies that orient investments exclusively to the home market will allow diminishing returns to capital accumulation to set in much more quickly. Sometimes luck, in the form of a terms-of-trade improvement or a resource discovery, will help. But, as in the Mauritian example of the early 1970s, good luck will have to be complemented with governmental efforts to channel resources into investments that diversify the economy.

Governments in countries with larger domestic markets can indulge in greater heterodoxy. Public investment—in infrastructure, irrigation, ports, and upstream industries—can often be a useful instrument for crowding in private investment, as the East Asian experience demonstrates. Experimentation with a certain dose of import-substitution policy in a few sectors of the economy may also prove productive, if it stimulates the animal spirits of domestic entrepreneurs. As I argue in the next chapter, the import-substitution policies followed in much of the developing world until the early 1980s were quite successful in some regards, and their costs have been greatly exaggerated.

I close this chapter with a clarification. My emphasis on the central role of investment should not be misunderstood as implying that all one needs to do to generate sustained growth is to step up the national investment effort. If that were the crux of the matter, centrally planned economies would have been the world's best performers over the longer run. Ultimately, the return to investment matters a great deal too. Rather, the key is to induce the private sector to invest by enhancing the perceived returns to private investments and to generate a virtuous cycle of profits, investments, and capacity expansion.[10] In practice, different countries have found different ways of triggering this process: they have used direct investment subsidies (South Korea and Taiwan), opened up profitable export opportunities (Mauritius), or provided a certain degree of protection in home markets (most countries with ISI policies). Successful cases are characterized neither by a hands-off approach with complete reliance on markets, nor by a strategy of command and control. Rather, they share a pragmatic approach built on the specific strengths of the domestic economy.

NOTES

[1] On Mauritius, see Wellisz and Saw (1993). The Nobelist is James Meade (Meade et al. 1961).

[2] According to Wellisz and Saw (1993) , this segmentation lasted until the mid-1980s.

[3] This account of East Asia draws on Rodrik (1995b, 1997a, 1998a forthcoming).

[4] These points are discussed at greater length in Rodrik (1995b). The evidence underlying the claims on the stability and timing of price incentives affecting exports comes from Frank, Kim, and Westphal (1975).

[5] The information in this paragraph is taken from Lin (1973, pp. 85-87) and Kuo (1983, p. 301).

[6] Young (1995) estimates TFP growth since the 1960s to have been 2.3 percent in Hong Kong and near zero (0.2 percent) in Singapore. The Collins-Bosworth (1996) estimate for Singapore is substantially higher (Table 1), although still undistinguished by comparative standards.

[7] For more information about the data provided from the Penn World Tables, see Appendix in this essay.

[8] Taiwan does not show up because Taiwanese data start in 1965, and the filter I have applied requires five years of observations prior to a candidate transition year before a transition can be identified.

[9] This analysis is inspired by Fischer, Sahay, and Vegh (1996), who applied a similar framework to the study of stabilization in former socialist economies.

[10] This is the sense in which an economy's investment rate is *endogenous*, determined in turn by other variables, including government policies. The short-run causality between investment and growth has not yet been fully sorted out in the literature. Blomstrom, Lipsey, and Zezan, (1996), for example, find that over five-year horizons investment tends to follow growth, rather than lead it. But such results are consistent with the argument in the text: policies (or other determinants) that enhance profitability will first show up in increased output.

Chapter 4
Managing Turbulence
in the World Economy

GETTING RECENT ECONOMIC
HISTORY STRAIGHT

■ THIS CHAPTER REVOLVES AROUND THE RECENT economic history of the developing countries. I begin by emphasizing the successful nature of their experience with growth until the late 1970s and then focus on the reasons for their subsequent dismal performance. Much of current orthodoxy is based on a misleading interpretation of this history. Getting the story straight is important not only from an academic standpoint but as a guide to future policy. I argue that what this history demonstrates is first and foremost the importance of maintaining macroeconomic stability in the face of a volatile external environment. Import-substitution policies themselves were not the root source of the decline in growth. Further, I show that it is the quality of the domestic institutions of conflict management that determines a country's capacity for macroeconomic adjustment. This perspective has implications for institutional reforms, ranging from the consolidation of democracy to the establishment of social insurance mechanisms.

THE GOLDEN PERIOD OF GROWTH

The postwar period up until 1973 was the golden era for economic growth. Scores of developing countries experienced rates of economic expansion that were virtually unprecedented in the history of the world economy. As Table 4.1 shows, there were no fewer than 42 developing countries whose economies grew at rates exceeding 2.5 percent per capita per annum from at least 1960 until the first oil shock hit. At this rate of growth, incomes would double every 28 years or less—that is, every generation. The list of countries with this enviable record goes far beyond the handful of usual East Asian suspects and covers all parts of the globe, including 12 countries in South America, six in the Middle East and North Africa, and even 15 in Sub-Saharan Africa. In fact, there were no fewer than six Sub-Saharan African countries among the 20 fastest-growing developing countries in the world prior to 1973: Swaziland, Botswana, Côte d'Ivoire, Lesotho, Gabon, and Togo, with Kenya ranking 21st. There were only 10 countries in the developing world (for which we have data) where per capita income failed to rise.[1]

Country	1960-1973*	1973-1984	1984-1994	1960-1994*
Oman	10.52	5.22	0.83	5.96
Taiwan, China	8.10	5.78	6.33	6.61
Singapore	6.90	5.54	5.09	5.93
Swaziland	6.74	0.14	0.16	2.67
Korea, Republic of	6.69	6.45	7.32	6.80
Hong Kong	6.18	5.54	4.66	5.41
Botswana	6.15	7.34	4.11	5.94
Côte d'Ivoire	5.63	-0.20	-3.88	0.95
Malta	5.22	7.19	n.a.	5.74
Barbados	5.22	1.13	1.34	2.76
Israel	5.03	1.45	2.37	3.09
Lesotho	4.94	1.75	3.80	3.57
Brazil	4.74	1.72	0.81	2.60
Gabon	4.72	0.43	-4.20	0.71
Thailand	4.49	3.93	7.21	5.10
Panama	4.46	1.74	0.44	2.40
Togo	4.17	-0.60	-2.42	0.69
Papua New Guinea	4.14	-1.51	3.04	1.99
Malaysia	4.09	4.50	3.87	4.16
Dominican Republic	3.77	1.66	1.05	2.29
Kenya	3.40	0.25	0.54	1.54
Fiji	3.19	0.50	1.52	1.83
Mexico	3.18	2.05	0.43	2.01
Mauritius	3.14	0.96	5.22	3.24
Pakistan	3.10	2.70	2.37	2.76
Costa Rica	3.02	0.15	1.84	1.74
Trinidad and Tobago	2.97	2.51	-2.45	1.23
Jamaica	2.97	-2.63	2.20	0.93
Burundi	2.95	0.86	-0.51	1.26
Turkey	2.94	1.67	1.87	2.21
Belize	2.91	2.37	3.80	3.00
Malawi	2.85	0.78	-1.98	0.76
Mauritania	2.85	-0.83	0.38	0.93
Bahamas	2.84	1.12	-0.47	1.31
Gambia	2.80	1.27	-1.33	1.09

Continued on next page

Country	1960-1973*	1973-1984	1984-1994	1960-1994*
Continued				
Guatemala	2.79	0.03	0.10	1.11
Nicaragua	2.71	-3.06	-4.67	-1.33
Seychelles	2.67	2.34	4.09	2.98
Egypt, Arab Rep.	2.64	6.05	0.33	3.06
Tanzania	2.64	-3.65	0.50	-0.03
Iraq	2.60	-0.93	n.a.	n.a.
Zimbabwe	2.58	-0.85	0.16	0.75
China	2.48	5.39	8.52	5.20
Congo	2.46	5.75	-3.69	1.72
Colombia	2.45	1.68	2.37	2.18
South Africa	2.39	0.19	-1.62	0.50
Argentina	2.29	-0.23	1.07	1.12
Peru	2.24	-0.66	-0.52	0.49
Bolivia	2.23	-0.70	0.32	0.72
Philippines	2.10	1.13	-0.10	1.13

Source: World Bank data.

*1965-1973 or 1965-1994 in some cases, where earlier data are not available.
Data for Mauritius are 1960-1976 and 1976-1984.

There can be little doubt that economic growth led to substantial improvements in the living conditions of the vast majority of the households in these countries. We can see the results in indicators of human development. Between 1967 and 1977, life expectancy at birth increased by four years in Brazil (from 58 to 62), by five years in Côte d'Ivoire (from 43 to 48), by five years in Mexico (from 60 to 65), and by five years in Pakistan (from 48 to 53). In Kenya, infant mortality fell from 112 per 1,000 live births in 1965 to 72 in 1980.[2]

Most of the countries that did well in this period followed import-substitution policies (ISI). These policies created protected and therefore profitable home markets for domestic entrepreneurs to invest in, and spurred growth.[3] Contrary to received wisdom, ISI-driven growth did not produce tremendous inefficiencies on an economywide scale. In fact, the productivity performance of many Latin American and Middle Eastern countries was, in comparative perspective, exemplary.

Table 4.2 shows averages for total factor productivity (TFP) growth for the three periods delineated in Table 4.1. As before, we look first only at the performance for the 1960-1973 period. The comparative evidence is rather striking: not only was average TFP growth during the period preceding the first oil shock quite high in the Middle East and Latin America (at 2.3 and 1.8 percent, respectively), it was actually significantly higher than in East Asia (1.3 percent). Countries such as Brazil, the Dominican Republic, and Ecuador in Latin America; Iran, Morocco, and Tunisia in the Middle East; and Côte d'Ivoire and Kenya in Africa all experienced faster TFP growth than any of the East Asian countries in this early period (with the possible exception of Hong Kong, for which comparable data are not available). Mexico, Bolivia, Panama, Egypt, Algeria, Tanzania, and Zaire experienced higher TFP growth than all but Taiwan. Of course, not all countries following ISI policies did well: Argentina is a striking counterexample, with an average TFP growth of only 0.2 percent during 1960-1973.[4]

Productivity growth estimates of this type are not without serious problems, and one can quibble with the methodologies employed (see Rodrik forthcoming 1998a for a critique). Nevertheless, there is little reason to believe that the estimates of Collins and Bosworth (1996) shown in Table 4.2 are seriously biased in the way that they rank different regions. The inescapable conclusion is that most of the countries in Latin America and the Middle East had productivity growth records prior to 1973 that look quite favorable in comparison with those in East Asia.

How do we square this evidence with the received wisdom that countries following the ISI strategy fell prey to myriad inefficiencies? The dismal reputation of ISI is due partly to the subsequent economic collapse experienced by many of its adherents in the 1980s, and partly to the influential studies of Little, Scitovsky, and Scott (1970) and Balassa and associates (1971). I discuss the collapse of the 1980s and its possible links to ISI in the next section. I say a few words about Little et al. and Balassa here.

What these two important studies did was to document in detail some of the static economic inefficiencies generated by high and extremely dispersed effective rates of protection (ERP) in the manufacturing sectors of the countries under study. The discovery of cases of negative value added at

	1960-73		1973-84		1984-94	
	GDP per worker	**TFP**	**GDP per worker**	**TFP**	**GDP per worker**	**TFP**
East Asia	4.2	1.3	4.0	0.5	4.4	1.6
Latin America	3.4	1.8	0.4	-1.1	0.1	-0.4
Middle East	4.7	2.3	0.5	-2.2	-1.1	-1.5
South Asia	1.8	0.1	2.5	1.2	2.7	1.5
Sub-Saharan Africa	1.9	0.3	-0.6	-2.0	-0.6	-0.4
East Asia						
China	2.2	1.4	4.3	2.2	8.0	4.6
Indonesia	2.5	1.1	4.3	0.5	3.7	0.9
South Korea	5.6	1.4	5.3	1.1	6.2	2.1
Malaysia	4.0	1.0	3.6	0.4	3.8	1.4
Philippines	2.5	0.7	1.2	-1.3	-0.3	-0.9
Singapore	5.9	0.9	4.3	1.0	6.0	3.1
Thailand	4.8	1.4	3.6	1.1	6.9	3.3
Taiwan	6.8	2.2	4.9	0.9	5.6	2.8
Latin America						
Argentina	2.6	0.2	0.4	-1.0	1.1	1.0
Bolivia	3.5	2.1	-0.6	-1.5	-0.1	0.8
Brazil	4.4	2.9	1.0	-0.8	0.5	-0.2
Chile	1.6	0.7	-0.6	-0.7	4.7	3.7
Colombia	2.9	1.9	1.2	0.0	1.8	1.0
Costa Rica	2.8	1.2	-0.5	-2.0	1.9	0.6
Dominican Rep.	4.6	2.5	0.8	-1.3	0.0	-1.0
Ecuador	4.4	3.3	1.7	-0.5	0.0	-0.1
Guatemala	3.2	1.9	0.5	-0.9	0.0	0.2
Guyana	0.4	0.2	-4.6	-4.3	-0.5	-0.3
Honduras	2.4	1.3	0.3	-1.1	-0.6	-1.2
Haiti	-0.2	-0.8	1.1	-1.5	-5.2	-5.2
Jamaica	3.3	1.5	-4.4	-4.0	0.6	0.8
Mexico	3.8	1.6	0.7	-0.8	-1.1	-1.8
Nicaragua	3.1	1.4	-3.2	-4.1	-5.7	-5.5
Panama	4.6	1.7	1.4	-0.2	-0.3	-0.6
Peru	2.6	1.4	-1.1	-2.2	-1.5	-1.3
Paraguay	2.0	0.8	3.1	0.0	0.6	-0.3
El Salvador	2.0	0.6	-2.4	-3.6	-0.2	-0.2
Trinidad and Tobago	3.3	2.0	3.9	1.2	-3.3	-2.8
Uruguay	0.4	0.1	0.5	-0.9	2.8	2.5
Venezuela	1.2	0.9	-3.1	-4.3	-0.6	-0.4

Continued on next page

TABLE 4.2. ECONOMIC PERFORMANCE BY PERIOD (annual average growth rates, in percent)

	1960-73		1973-84		1984-94	
	GDP per worker	TFP	GDP per worker	TFP	GDP per worker	TFP
Continued						
Middle East						
Cyprus	3.9	1.4	5.6	4.0	4.8	3.5
Algeria	2.3	1.6	2.4	-0.1	-3.3	-3.3
Egypt	3.0	1.8	6.2	2.3	0.0	-1.5
Iran	6.1	2.4	-2.9	-5.7	-2.2	-2.2
Israel	5.1	3.3	1.2	-0.1	2.7	1.9
Jordan	2.1	-0.9	6.7	2.3	-1.2	-2.9
Morocco	4.7	3.5	1.3	-0.5	0.9	0.3
Malta	3.7	1.9	6.6	4.9	3.9	2.0
Tunisia	4.1	2.3	2.2	0.2	0.7	0.1
South Asia						
Bangladesh	0.0	-0.6	2.5	1.8	1.1	0.7
India	1.8	0.1	2.4	1.0	3.1	1.6
Sri Lanka	2.1	1.0	3.2	0.7	2.7	1.0
Myanmar	0.5	0.1	3.5	1.9	-0.6	-1.6
Pakistan	3.9	0.2	2.8	2.0	2.7	1.5
Sub-Saharan Africa						
Côte d'Ivoire	5.9	3.3	0.5	-2.0	-2.4	-1.8
Cameroon	0.6	-0.8	6.7	3.4	-4.5	-5.7
Ethiopia	2.2	0.2	0.0	-0.9	-0.2	-1.6
Ghana	0.9	-1.0	-3.2	-3.2	1.8	1.1
Kenya	3.4	3.4	0.4	-0.1	0.1	0.4
Madagascar	0.3	-0.4	-2.0	-2.2	-0.9	-1.0
Mali	1.2	0.4	0.3	-0.2	0.9	0.4
Mozambique	2.9	1.1	-7.7	-7.1	3.5	3.0
Mauritius	1.5	1.5	1.0	0.3	4.0	2.8
Malawi	3.3	0.2	1.5	0.0	-1.1	-0.8
Nigeria	1.2	-0.9	-2.3	-4.6	1.3	2.0
Rwanda	-0.2	-0.8	1.7	-0.1	-3.6	-4.3
Sudan	-1.4	-3.7	2.1	0.2	-0.7	-0.7
Senegal	-0.5	-0.6	0.0	-0.2	0.2	-0.2
Sierra Leone	3.4	1.3	0.9	0.2	-0.3	-0.2
Uganda	0.7	-0.3	-2.9	-3.0	1.3	1.1
Tanzania	3.0	2.2	-1.1	-1.7	1.0	0.6
South Africa	2.3	0.9	1.0	-0.3	-2.0	-1.8
Zaire	2.4	2.2	-2.2	-3.4	-5.2	-5.9
Zambia	1.0	0.2	-2.3	-1.9	-2.5	-1.1
Zimbabwe	2.9	2.7	-0.8	-1.3	0.2	0.4

Source: Collins and Bosworth (1996) and personal communication from Susan Collins. I am grateful to Collins for making the individual country data available.

world prices—that is, cases in which countries would have been better off throwing away the inputs than processing them as they did in highly protected plants—was a particular shocker. However, neither study claimed to show that countries that had followed "outward-oriented" strategies had been systematically immune from the same kind of inefficiencies. In fact, the evidence can be read as suggesting that there was no such clear dividing line. For example, the figures provided by Little et al. (1970, pp. 174-190) show Taiwan to have had a higher average ERP in manufacturing, as well as greater variation in ERPs, than Mexico, long after Taiwan's trade reforms were introduced. This is significant, given that we commonly think of these two countries as exemplars of two diametrically opposed styles of development. Moreover, the systematic evidence on TFP growth reviewed above belies the idea that ISI produced more dynamic inefficiency than "outward orientation."[5]

Hence, as a strategy of industrialization intended to increase domestic investment and enhance productivity, import substitution apparently worked well in a very broad range of countries until at least the mid-1970s. Warts and all, ISI achieved a more than respectable record. In terms of the discussion in the previous chapter, ISI was a successful "investment strategy." Had the world come to an end in 1973, ISI would never have acquired its dismal reputation; nor would East Asia have earned its "miracle" appellation.[6]

OIL SHOCKS AND DEBT CRISES: THE WATERSHED YEARS

History, however, continued past 1973, and a disaster befell the vast majority of the economies that had been doing well. Of the 42 countries with growth rates above 2.5 percent prior to 1973, fewer than a third (12) managed the same record over the next decade (see Table 4.1). The median growth rate for all developing countries fell from 2.6 percent during 1960-1973 to 0.9 percent during 1973-1984 and to 0.8 percent during 1984-1994. The dispersion in performance across developing countries increased sharply, with the coefficient of variation for national growth rates increasing threefold after 1973 (see Table 4.3).

Perhaps nothing tells the story in as striking terms as the evidence on TFP growth. The Middle East and Latin America, which had led the

TABLE 4.3. SUMMARY STATISTICS FOR GROWTH RATES OF PER CAPITA GDP (all developing countries, percent)

	1960-1973	1973-1984	1984-1994	1960-1994
Mean	2.52	0.99	0.94	1.62
Median	2.59	0.86	0.81	1.23
Coefficient of variation across countries	0.91	2.89	3.12	1.26

Source: Calculated from World Bank data.

developing world in TFP growth prior to 1973, not only fell behind, but actually experienced *negative* TFP growth on average thereafter (see Table 4.2). In Sub-Saharan Africa, where productivity growth had been undistinguished but still positive, TFP growth turned negative as well. As Table 4.2 shows, East Asia held its own, while South Asia actually improved its performance.

This was not the result of the "exhaustion" of import-substitution policies (whatever that term actually means). Rather, the common timing implicates the turbulence that beset the world economy following 1973—the abandonment of the Bretton Woods system of fixed exchange rates, two major oil shocks, various other commodity boom-and-bust cycles, plus the interest rate shock of the early 1980s brought on by the tight-money policies of Federal Reserve Chair Paul Volcker. The fact that some of the most ardent followers of ISI policies in South Asia (India and Pakistan in particular) managed either to hold on to their growth rates after 1973 (Pakistan) or increase them (India) also suggests that more than just ISI was involved.

The actual story is straightforward. The proximate reason for the economic collapse was the inability to adjust macroeconomic policies appropriately in the wake of these external shocks. Macroeconomic maladjustment gave rise to a range of syndromes associated with macroeconomic instability—high or repressed inflation, scarcity of foreign exchange and large black-market premiums, external-payments imbalances and debt crises—that greatly magnified the real costs of the shocks. The evidence in Figure 4.1 demonstrates this point clearly. There was a strong association between inflation and black-market premiums and the magnitude of economic collapse

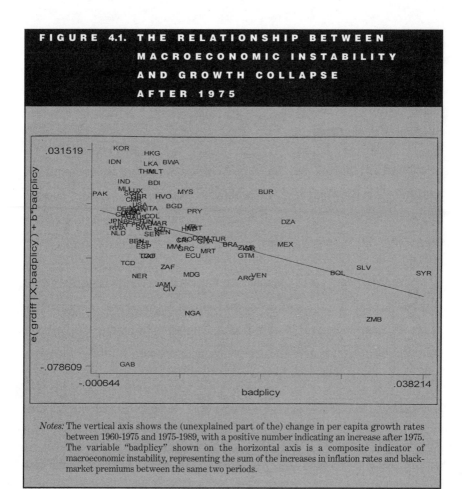

FIGURE 4.1. THE RELATIONSHIP BETWEEN MACROECONOMIC INSTABILITY AND GROWTH COLLAPSE AFTER 1975

Notes: The vertical axis shows the (unexplained part of the) change in per capita growth rates between 1960-1975 and 1975-1989, with a positive number indicating an increase after 1975. The variable "badplicy" shown on the horizontal axis is a composite indicator of macroeconomic instability, representing the sum of the increases in inflation rates and black-market premiums between the same two periods.

experienced in different countries. The countries that suffered the most were those with the largest increases in inflation and black-market premiums for foreign currency. The culprits were poor monetary and fiscal policies and inadequate adjustments in exchange-rate policy, sometimes aggravated by shortsighted policies of creditors, the IMF, and the World Bank.[7]

It is true that many, if not most, of the countries that had embarked on ISI strategies in the 1960s became the casualties of the debt crisis and related macrosyndromes. This is what makes the association between ISI strategies and growth collapses plausible on the face of it. But there are problems with this interpretation. There are no good arguments explaining why a set of *microeconomic* policies, such as the ISI policies, should have been necessarily and systematically associated with *macroeconomic disequilibrium*, which is what the debt crisis represented (see the discussion in Rodrik 1996b). In any case, it is clear that there was nothing preordained about the debt crisis: some of the countries that adhered most rigidly to ISI policies—India being a chief example—were able to avoid protracted debt crises. Indeed, as Table 4.2 shows, the only region of the world that experienced a significant rise in TFP growth after 1973 was, in fact, South Asia—that is, Bangladesh, India, Burma (Myanmar), Pakistan, and Sri Lanka—which is not exactly the region that comes to mind when one thinks of "outward orientation."

The point is made somewhat more systematically in Table 4.4, taken from Rodrik (1996b) and based on information from Little et al. (1993) and Easterly (1993). The table evaluates the relevance of three types of potential explanations for whether a country succumbed to the 1982 debt crisis or not: 1) the magnitude of the external shock, 2) the adjustments in monetary and fiscal policies, and 3) the extent of microeconomic policy distortions. The results point unambiguously to macroeconomic policies as the chief culprit. *All* the countries that Little et al. classify as having been "troubled" are also classified as cases of "failure to adjust monetary and fiscal policy." *None* of the "untroubled" countries are similarly classified. With regard to price distortions, these were on average no higher (in fact, somewhat lower) in the "troubled" countries than in the "untroubled" countries. Likewise, there is no clear-cut pattern where external shocks are concerned.

The bottom line is that in those countries that experienced a debt crisis, the crisis was the product of monetary and fiscal policies that were incompatible with sustainable external balances: there was too little expenditure reducing and expenditure switching. Trade and industrial policies had little to do with bringing on the crisis.

. . . .

WHERE DOES THE ABILITY TO ADJUST MACROPOLICIES COME FROM?

■   WHY WERE SOME COUNTRIES QUICKER to adjust their macroeconomic policies than others? The deeper determinants of growth performance after the 1970s are rooted in the ability of domestic institutions to manage the distributional conflicts triggered by the external shocks of the period.

TABLE 4.4. DETERMINANTS OF THE DEBT
CRISIS, 1982

	Large external shock	Failure to adjust monetary and fiscal policy	Large microeconomic distortions
Troubled Countries			
Argentina	No	Yes	Yes
Brazil	Yes	Yes	No
Chile	Yes	Yes	Yes
Costa Rica	No	Yes	Yes
Côte d'Ivoire	Yes	Yes	No
Mexico	No	Yes	n.a.
Morocco	No	Yes	Yes
Nigeria	No	Yes	No
Moderately Troubled Countries			
Colombia	No	Yes	Yes
Kenya	Yes	Yes	No
Sri Lanka	Yes	No	Yes
Untroubled Countries			
Cameroon	Yes	No	No
India	No	No	Yes
Indonesia	No	No	Yes
Korea	Yes	No	No
Pakistan	No	No	Yes
Thailand	Yes	No	n.a.
Turkey	No	No	n.a.

Source: Little et al. (1993), Table 4.4, except for the relative-price distortion index, which is taken from Easterly (1993). The latter index is the variance of the log input prices (relative to U.S. prices) across commodities, measured in 1980. "Yes" > 0.26.

SHOCKS, MACROPOLICIES, AND SOCIAL CONFLICTS

Think of an economy that is suddenly and unexpectedly confronted with a drop in the price of its main export (or a sudden reversal of capital flows). The textbook prescription for this economy is a combination of expenditure-switching and expenditure-reducing policies—that is, a devaluation and fiscal retrenchment. But the precise manner in which these policy changes are administered can have significant distributional implications.

Should the devaluation be accompanied by wage controls? Should import tariffs be raised? Should the fiscal retrenchment be carried out through spending cuts or tax increases? If spending is to be cut, which types of expenditures should bear the brunt of the cuts? Should interest rates be raised to rein in private spending as well?

In general, macroeconomic theory does not have a clear preference among the available options. But because each of the options has predictable distributional consequences, in practice much depends on the severity of the social conflicts that lie beneath the surface. If the appropriate adjustments can be undertaken without an outbreak of distributional conflict or without upsetting prevailing social bargains, the shock can be managed with few long-lasting effects on the economy. If they cannot, the economy can be paralyzed for years, as inadequate adjustment condemns the country to foreign-exchange bottlenecks, import compression, debt crises, and bouts of high inflation. Furthermore, deep social divisions provide an incentive to governments to delay needed adjustments and take on excessive levels of foreign debt, in the expectation that other social groups can be made to pay for the eventual costs.

Consider, for example, the experiences of three countries, all of which were hit by sizable terms-of-trade shocks during the mid-to-late 1970s: South Korea, Turkey, and Brazil. Among these three, South Korea suffered the greatest external shock, because trade constitutes a much larger share of national income there, and, consequently, the income loss associated with a rise in the price of imported oil was correspondingly larger. Yet South Korea grew even faster after the mid-1970s, while Turkey and Brazil both experienced an economic collapse.

SOUTH KOREA. At one level, it is not a great mystery why the experiences of the three countries differ. In addition to greater dependence on oil imports, South Korea's troubles in 1980 were exacerbated by an unusually poor harvest, which alone accounted for a three percent decline in GDP (Maddison 1985). However, as soon as signs of a payments imbalance appeared, the South Korean government, with help from the IMF, undertook a textbook adjustment in 1980 consisting of three main parts.

First, in January 1980, the South Korean government devalued the won by 17 percent. This devaluation, along with a new, more flexible exchange-rate policy, led to an overall decline in the won of seven percent in real terms by the end of 1980 (Aghevli and Marquez-Ruarte 1985). Second, for the first half of 1980, the government tightened monetary policy, particularly credit policy, which caused the growth of both bank credit and the broad money supply to decline sharply. (A rather acute recession prompted South Korean authorities to relax credit policy in the latter half of 1980). The third part of South Korea's adjustment came in the form of a program aimed at increasing energy efficiency in the economy, specifically by making South Korea's economy less dependent on imported oil. This was no small task, since in 1979 oil accounted for 63 percent of South Korea's domestic energy consumption. The government achieved its energy efficiency objectives in part by raising the price of oil 230 percent and in part through changes in the exchange rate. In addition, the program included mandates for reduced electricity consumption by nonessential activities, such as the use of elevators and air-conditioning (Aghevli and Marquez-Ruarte 1985).

South Korea experienced a reduction in GDP growth of five percent in 1980. But largely because the expenditure-reduction and expenditure-switching policies were implemented rapidly and decisively, the economy avoided a protracted crisis. Growth resumed soon thereafter.

TURKEY. The Turkish response was quite different. A populist government reacted to the growing current-account deficit in the mid-1970s by going on an unsustainable external borrowing binge. The government subsidized private-sector foreign borrowing by providing blanket protection against foreign-exchange risk. Once foreign bank loans dried up (during 1977-78, as a result of concerns about repayment capacity), fiscal and exchange-rate adjustments were delayed.

The result was that the inflation rate rose and the economy went into a tailspin between 1978 and 1980. Some semblance of macroeconomic balance was restored in 1980, when Turgut Özal implemented a stabilization package supported by the IMF. The program relied on large changes in key relative prices (the real exchange rate, real wages, and the rural-urban terms of trade), with huge distributional consequences. These relative-price changes had the effect of transferring income from farmers and workers to the public sector (see Celasun and Rodrik 1989). They were greatly facilitated by the fact that military rule during 1980-83 kept protest from popular sectors in check.

These distributional shifts have created a legacy of macroeconomic cycles in Turkey, with real wages going through periods of recovery followed by bust. Largely because of this legacy of instability, inflation has remained high since the early 1980s, and the Turkish economy has underperformed relative to its potential.

BRAZIL. In Brazil, widespread indexation prevented an adjustment in relative prices of the kind that eventually took place in Turkey. Even without *formal* indexation, strategic interaction among social groups resulting in wage-price rigidities appears to have made orthodox adjustment policies of demand restraint extremely costly in terms of output (Simonsen 1988). Consequently, fiscal and monetary restraint was tried only halfheartedly. The result was an alternation between various currency reform plans and a succession of high-inflation plateaus.

Inflation jumped from 50 percent per year to 100 percent in 1979, and then to 200 percent in 1983, where it stayed until the implementation of the Cruzado Plan in February 1986, which froze the new currency's value at 1,000 units of the former currency. This first attempt at restraint lasted until the end of the year, after which inflation again exploded, to 400 percent in 1987, 1000 percent in 1988, and more than 2000 percent in 1990. Each failed stabilization resulted in higher inflation rates than previously, until the "real plan" of 1994 (which took its name from Brazil's relabeled unit of currency) finally brought price stability. Introduced by Minister of Finance Fernando Henrique Cardoso (who was elected Brazil's president in 1994), the real plan avoided the drastic measures of the previous attempts and instead focused on reducing prices by pegging the real to the dollar, thereby reducing inflationary expectations.

DISCUSSION. These country stories underscore the importance of the manner in which different societies react to external shocks. In South Korea, adjustment was swift and somehow nonpoliticized. In Turkey, adjustment was delayed, and when it eventually took place, it was undertaken in a manner that imposed disproportionate costs on certain segments of society, undercutting the sustainability of macrobalances in the longer run. In Brazil, strategic competition among different social groups gave prices a life of their own and rendered traditional remedies for excess demand costly and ineffective.

In short, social conflicts and their management—whether successful or not—played a key role in how the effects of external shocks were transmitted to economic performance. I believe that this is a key insight into economic performance and the manner in which the global economy impinges on it. Societies that benefit most from integration into the world economy are those that have the complementary institutions at home that manage and contain the conflicts that economic interdependence can trigger.

CROSS-NATIONAL EVIDENCE

Societies with deep social cleavages and poor institutions of conflict management tend not to be very good at handling shocks. In such societies, the economic costs of exogenous shocks—such as deteriorations in the terms of trade—are magnified by the distributional conflicts that are triggered by these shocks. Such conflicts diminish the productivity with which a society's resources are utilized in a number of ways: by delaying needed adjustments in fiscal policies and key relative prices (such as the real exchange rate or real wages) and by diverting activities away from the productive and entrepreneurial spheres. As in Rodrik (1998b), the central idea can be summarized heuristically by the following formula:

$$\Delta \, growth = - \, external \, shocks \times \frac{latent \, social \, conflict}{institutions \, of \, conflict \, management}$$

The effect of shocks on growth is larger, the greater the latent social conflicts in an economy and the weaker its institutions of conflict management.

In Rodrik (1998b), I used various proxies for the terms on the right side of the equation to provide empirical support for the ideas. I measured external shocks by calculating the income effects of the volatility of the external terms of trade. I proxied for "latent social conflict" by using measures of inequality and ethnic and linguistic fragmentation. Most important, I proxied "institutions of conflict management" by using measures of democracy, the rule of law, and public spending on social insurance. I provide an overview of some of the key results in the following paragraphs.

Figures 4.2 through 4.6 display the partial correlations across countries between the reduction in growth after 1975 and various indicators of social conflict and institutions. In each case, the dependent variable (shown on the vertical axis) is the difference in per capita growth rates between the two periods 1960-1975 and 1975-1989. (A positive number indicates higher growth in the later period.) The following controls have been included in each regression, in addition to the variable of interest: growth during 1960-1975 (to control for convergence), log per capita GDP in 1975 (to control for other structural characteristics of economies that may be related to sensitivity to shocks), and regional dummies for Latin America, East Asia, and Sub-Saharan Africa (to rule out spurious correlation arising from purely geographical effects). Hence, the scatter plots represent the association between the variables on the axes *after* controlling for these other influences.

Figures 4.2 and 4.3 show that there is a strong statistical relationship between indicators of latent conflict and growth declines following external shocks. Countries with greater income inequalities during the 1970s (*gini70*) had larger reductions in economic growth. The estimated coefficient suggests that a 10-point difference in the Gini scale (roughly the difference between Brazil and Costa Rica, or half the difference between Turkey and Taiwan) contributed a reduction in growth of 1.3 percentage points. The evidence on ethnic and linguistic fragmentation is similar (Figure 4.3). The indicator used here (*elf60*) comes from Mauro (1995) and measures the likelihood that any two randomly drawn individuals in a society will not belong to the same ethnic and linguistic group. There is a strong and statistically significant relationship between fragmentation according to this measure and the extent of growth collapse after 1975. Hence, countries with more divided societies—whether the divisions lie along income lines or ethnic lines—do a poor job of handling shocks.

The more encouraging results from the exercise relate to the role played by institutions, which, in principle, can be improved. Figure 4.4 shows that the rule of law and the quality of governmental institutions make a significant difference, and can override latent conflict and divisions. The indicator used in Figure 4.4 is Knack and Keefer's (1995) measure of institutional quality (*icrge*), which derives from the International Country Risk Guide. A one-point increase in this indicator (which is measured on a scale of 1 to 10) is estimated to increase growth (relative to the earlier period) by 0.6 percent.

Perhaps a more unexpected result is that democracy helps too (Figure 4.5). There is a strong association between various measures of democracy and relative economic performance since 1975. Figure 4.5 shows the results with the Freedom House indicator of civil liberties and political rights (*democ70s*, rescaled from zero to one, with an increase corresponding to improvement in democratic rights). An increase in this indicator of 0.5 points during the 1970s (roughly the difference between Costa Rica and Mexico) is estimated to have increased post-1975 growth by one percentage point relative to earlier growth. This result holds across alternative data sets using different indicators of democratic procedures. Figure 4.6, for example,

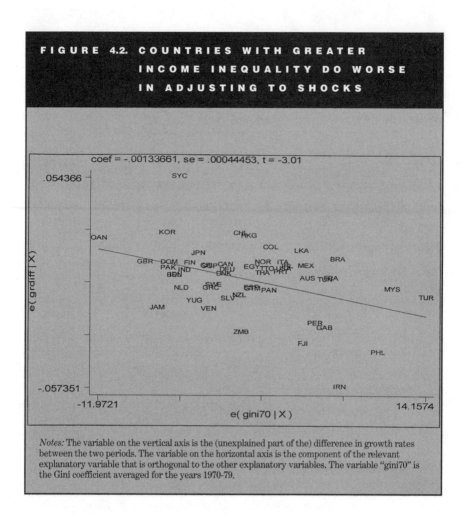

FIGURE 4.2. COUNTRIES WITH GREATER INCOME INEQUALITY DO WORSE IN ADJUSTING TO SHOCKS

coef = -.00133661, se = .00044453, t = -3.01

Notes: The variable on the vertical axis is the (unexplained part of the) difference in growth rates between the two periods. The variable on the horizontal axis is the component of the relevant explanatory variable that is orthogonal to the other explanatory variables. The variable "gini70" is the Gini coefficient averaged for the years 1970-79.

shows a similar exercise with an indicator that quantifies the degree of access by nonelites to political institutions during the second half of the 1970s (*parcom_x*, calibrated on a scale of zero to one, and taken from Jaggers and Gurr 1995). I find that countries with more participatory political systems were generally better at handling the consequences of the shocks of the 1970s.

These kinds of results are not surprising once one looks at democracy from the perspective adopted here: democratic institutions are the institutions of conflict management par excellence. Democracy allows discredited policies and politicians to be discarded, it allows for institutionalized modes of participation instead of riots and protests, and it reduces incentives for

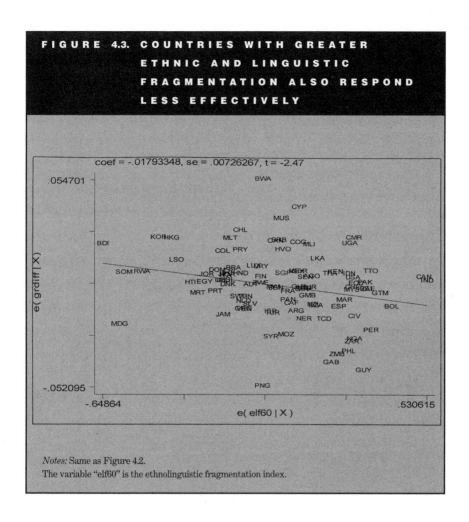

FIGURE 4.3. COUNTRIES WITH GREATER ETHNIC AND LINGUISTIC FRAGMENTATION ALSO RESPOND LESS EFFECTIVELY

coef = -.01793348, se = .00726267, t = -2.47

Notes: Same as Figure 4.2.
The variable "elf60" is the ethnolinguistic fragmentation index.

noncooperative behavior by making it harder for social groups to shift the burdens of adjustment disproportionately on to others (Rodrik 1998b). I discuss the role of democracy more extensively below.

There is also some suggestive evidence that societies that provide their citizens with greater amounts of social insurance tend to be better positioned to deal with shocks. Comprehensive and comparable measures of social insurance are, of course, difficult to come by. In Figure 4.7, I use a crude indicator, the logarithm of government expenditures on social security and welfare as a share of GDP averaged over the period 1975-79 (*lss7579*). The results are suggestive: there is a positive and statistically significant

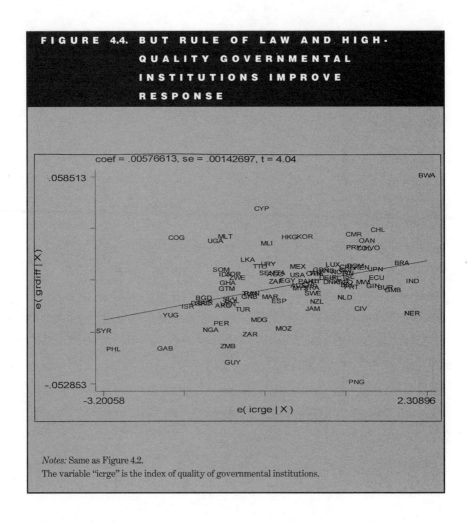

Notes: Same as Figure 4.2.
The variable "icrge" is the index of quality of governmental institutions.

relationship between spending on social safety nets and relative performance after 1975. Although more evidence is certainly needed, these results are supportive of the positive role played by social insurance in managing shocks and social conflict.

Finally, I show in Table 4.5 that the social conflict indicators I have considered here tend to be strongly correlated with the incidence of macroeconomic disequilibrium after 1975. Toward this purpose, I have constructed an indicator of macroeconomic disequilibrium for each country, taking a linear combination of the increase in the inflation rates and black-market premiums for foreign currency between the two periods. The weights on each component of the indicator are selected such that a unit increase

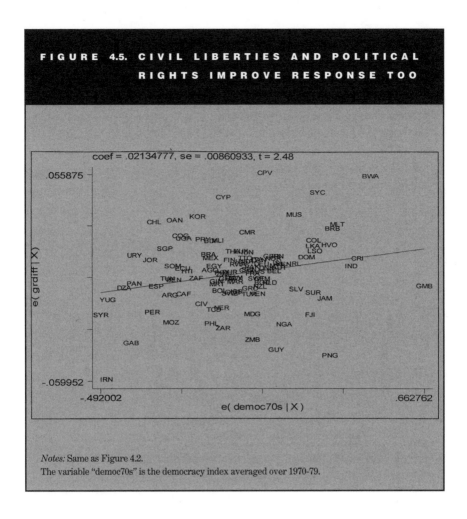

FIGURE 4.5. CIVIL LIBERTIES AND POLITICAL RIGHTS IMPROVE RESPONSE TOO

coef = .02134777, se = .00860933, t = 2.48

Notes: Same as Figure 4.2.
The variable "democ70s" is the democracy index averaged over 1970-79.

in this indicator is associated with a one percentage point decline in growth. This particular result is shown in column 1 of Table 4.5. Note that the estimated coefficient on macroeconomic disequilibrium is highly significant (with a *t*-statistic exceeding six), and thus bears out the argument made above regarding the critical role played by macroeconomic adjustment.

The remaining columns in Table 4.5 show that macroeconomic disequilibrium was more likely in countries with high degrees of income inequality and ethnolinguistic fragmentation, and less likely in countries with democratic institutions or high-quality government bureaucracies. All of these results are statistically significant at the 95 percent level

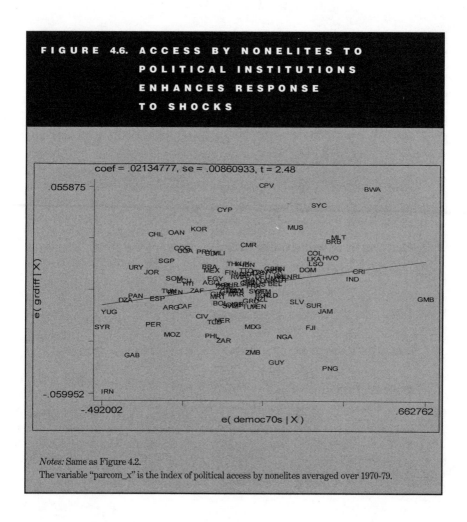

FIGURE 4.6. ACCESS BY NONELITES TO POLITICAL INSTITUTIONS ENHANCES RESPONSE TO SHOCKS

coef = .02134777, se = .00860933, t = 2.48

Notes: Same as Figure 4.2.
The variable "parcom_x" is the index of political access by nonelites averaged over 1970-79.

or better, except in the case of *elf60*. These findings confirm the importance of the institutions of conflict management in maintaining macroeconomic stability.

The bottom line is that this broader perspective helps us to understand the growth collapse that was the fate of so many countries after the 1970s. Countries that experienced the sharpest drops in GDP growth after 1975 were those with divided societies and weak institutions of conflict management. Once latent social conflict and the quality of conflict management institutions are taken into account, various measures of government policy at the outset of the crisis, such as openness to trade, microeconomic distortions, and the size of the public sector, contribute practically nothing

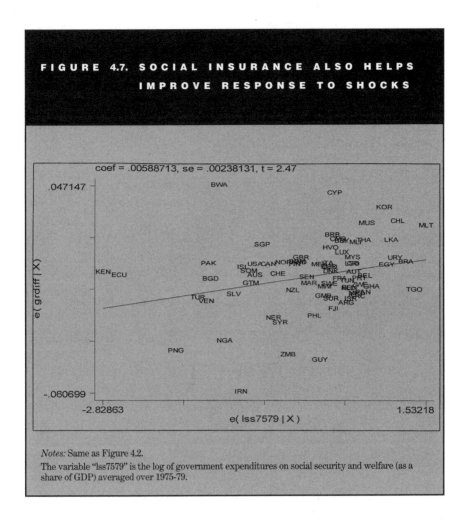

FIGURE 4.7. SOCIAL INSURANCE ALSO HELPS IMPROVE RESPONSE TO SHOCKS

Notes: Same as Figure 4.2.
The variable "lss7579" is the log of government expenditures on social security and welfare (as a share of GDP) averaged over 1975-79.

to explaining economic performance after 1975 (relative to the earlier period; see Rodrik 1998c).

· ·

SHOCKS REDUX: MANAGING THE ASIAN FINANCIAL CRISIS AND THE VIRTUES OF DEMOCRACY

■   IN 1996, FIVE ASIAN ECONOMIES (South Korea, Indonesia, Malaysia, Thailand, and the Philippines) received net private capital inflows amounting to $93.0 billion. One year later (in 1997), they experienced an estimated *out-flow* of $12.1 billion (IIF 1998), a turnaround in a single year of $105 billion, amounting to more than 10 percent of the combined GDP of these economies. By 1998, three of these economies (Indonesia, Thailand, and South Korea) were mired in a severe economic crisis, the magnitude of which would have seemed inconceivable even to the most knowledgeable and insightful observers of the region just months before.

THREE LESSONS OF THE ASIAN CRISIS

One lesson of the crisis is that international capital markets do a poor job of discriminating between good and bad risks. It is hard to believe that there was much collective rationality in investor behavior during and prior to the crisis: financial markets got it badly wrong either in 1996, when they poured money into the region, or in 1997, when they pulled back en masse. The implication is that relying excessively on liquid, short-term capital (as all of the three worst-affected countries did) is a dangerous strategy.

Second, the crisis has demonstrated that trade orientation per se has little to do with the propensity to be hit with severe liquidity problems. The Asian economies most affected by the reversal in capital flows were among the most outward oriented in the world, routinely pointed out as examples for other countries to follow. The determinants of the crisis—as with the debt crisis of 1982 and the Mexican peso crisis of 1994—were financial and macroeconomic. Trade and industrial policies were, at best, secondary factors.[8]

In keeping with the general theme of this chapter, a third lesson of the crisis is that domestic institutions of conflict management are critical in containing the adverse economic consequences of the initial shock. At the onset of the crisis, it seemed that authoritarian governments would have a better chance of preventing the social explosions that the crisis might create, while "messy" democracies would suffer. In fact, many critics of Western-style liberal democracy viewed the Thai and South Korean troubles in the early stages of the crisis—and the apparent Indonesian resolve—as an illustration of the economic superiority of governments based on so-called Asian values. The outcome has been quite the opposite. Indonesia, an ethnically divided society ruled by an autocracy, eventually descended into chaos, with a reduction in GDP predicted at 20 percent or more. South Korea and

Thailand's democratic institutions, and their practices of consultation and cooperation among social partners, made these countries much more adept at generating the requisite policy adjustments. Although neither of the two economies was out of the woods as of late 1998, their experience has demonstrated the importance of institutions, and of democratic institutions in particular, in dealing with external shocks.

WHY THAILAND AND SOUTH KOREA COPED WELL

Even though democratic institutions developed relatively recently in Thailand and South Korea, they helped these two countries adjust to the

TABLE 4.5. DETERMINANTS OF MACROECONOMIC DISEQUILIBRIUM

| | Dependent variable | | | | |
| | Difference in growth between two periods | Index of macro-maladjustment | | | |
	(1)	(2)	(3)	(4)	(5)
Index of macro-maladjustment	-1.00 (0.16)				
Gini coefficient, 1970s		0.04* (0.01)			
ELF60			0.27 (0.28)		
Democracy, 1970s				-0.99** (0.49)	
Institutions (ICRG)					-0.33* (0.09)
N	79	42	82	79	72
R²	0.63	0.71	0.16	0.36	0.48

Notes: Robust standard errors reported in parenthesis. Levels of statistical significance indicated by asterisks: *99 percent; **95 percent; ***90 percent. Additional explanatory variables not shown here: growth, 1960-75; log GDP per capita, 1975; a measure of external shocks, 1970s (except in col. 1); and regional dummies. "Index of macro-maladjustment" represents a linear combination of the increase in rates of inflation and black-market premiums over the two periods. Sample sizes differ according to the availability of data.

crisis in a number of ways.[9] First, they facilitated a smooth transfer of power from a discredited set of politicians to a new group of government leaders. Second, democracy imposed mechanisms of participation, consultation, and bargaining, enabling policymakers to fashion the consensus needed to undertake the necessary policy adjustments decisively. Third, because democracy provides for institutionalized mechanisms of "voice," the South Korean and Thai institutions obviated the need for riots, protests, and other kinds of disruptive actions by affected groups, and, furthermore, undercut support for such behavior by other groups in society.

In Thailand, Prime Minister Chavalit Yongchaiyudh resigned on November 6, 1997, shortly after "several hundred white-collar workers led demonstrations in Bangkok" (Bell 1998), and one month after the adoption of a new, anticorruption constitution. Three days later, an eight-party coalition led by Chuan Leekpai managed to obtain a majority of votes in parliament. News articles about Thailand abound with stories illustrating the willingness of the Thai people to give the new government the benefit of the doubt in the belief that the government has their best interest in mind. Chuan's new finance minister, Tarrin Nimmanahaeminda, related a story to the press about a letter he received from "a young Thai girl wishing him well in his efforts to turn around the economy and enclosing a 20-baht note that she had taken from her father's wallet—her contribution toward paying off the International Monetary Fund" (Rahul 1998 p.21). The government savings bank started a program under which people can open accounts designed to ameliorate the situation for those particularly hard hit by the crisis—a campaign referred to as "Thais helping Thais" (*The Economist* 1998a p.38). In a more nationalistic effort, the government has also tried to cushion the employment loss to its own citizens by expelling thousands of foreign workers (particularly the large number of Burmese working there), to demonstrate that "the government is doing its best to protect the livelihoods of its own people" (*The Economist* 1998a p.38). As instability has grown in Indonesia, Thailand's currency has strengthened. The IMF has suggested that Thailand might emerge as the leader in recovery from the "Asian flu." Thailand's relative success thus far in weathering this economic crisis has come, in Chuan's words, from "the utility of a democratic process that gives people the right to choose a government they believe can solve their problems" (Larimer, McCarthy, and Leekpai 1998 p.16).

In South Korea, Kim Dae Jung, veteran opposition leader of the National Congress for New Politics, ended the former ruling party's half-century of political dominance on December 19, becoming the first opposition candidate ever elected president in South Korean history. As in Thailand, the transition eased political tensions and brought in a new team that was not tainted or constrained by previous policies and commitments. Kim has cultivated an alliance with the working classes and the poor and made a strong commitment to furthering a clean democracy. To this end, he has made an effort to make sure that the people of South Korea feel that their voices are being heard. In January 1998 he began hosting "town meetings," in much the same manner as President Bill Clinton in the United States, increasing the accessibility of the president to the people (Cummings 1998 p.15). Kim has also been working with labor unions on the expansion of social safety nets in the form of welfare programs and increased opportunities for job training for the unemployed.

Kim was able to hold off labor unrest for an extended period by carefully discussing all potential changes and plans for restructuring with union leaders. In fact, some threatened strikes, such as the one by the Korean Confederation of Trade Unions (KCTU), planned for mid-February 1998 to protest a proposed labor reform law (to end lifetime employment by allowing firms to lay off workers in certain circumstances), were called off by the unions themselves, so as not to "endanger the nation's fragile economic recovery" (*Financial Times* 1998 p.2). By mid-April 1998, as the effects of the layoffs started to be felt, strike action increased as well. Despite efforts by the government to negotiate with unions, a nationwide strike called on May 27, 1998, by workers demanding more job security brought the South Korean stock market to its the lowest point in 11 years, a symptom of the mounting tension over the country's labor troubles. However, it is estimated that less than 20 percent of the trade unions' members have taken part in the strike, and it is also the case that, at least as of late 1998, the labor action had remained peaceful. South Korea has since begun a second round of labor talks (but without the KCTU). Meanwhile, South Korean citizens have hurried to turn in their gold jewelry to boost the foreign reserves, and businesses are conserving electricity by allowing elevators to stop on alternate floors only.

WHY INDONESIA COPED POORLY

This sense of shared sacrifice and compromise has been conspicuous in Indonesia by its absence. The financial difficulties spawned by the economic crisis were exacerbated by President Suharto's unwillingness to relinquish power, the lack of voice mechanisms (such as independent parties and free trade unions), and a generalized sense that the costs of the crisis would be passed on to the workers and the poor. Anti-Suharto sentiment welled up and exploded in the form of riots, looting, and other violence, some of it aimed at the country's ethnic Chinese minority. To divert blame from the government, some officials apparently incited ethnic tensions. According to one human rights group, instead of trying to prevent ethnic unrest, some "senior officials ... have tried to deflect blame for the economic crisis on to prominent members of the ethnic Chinese community" (cited in *The Economist* 1998b p.46). A student demonstration on May 12, 1998, during which soldiers shot and killed six protesters, snowballed into massive protests, culminating in Suharto's reluctant departure from power. The outgoing president handpicked his successor, however, one of his closest associates, B. J. Habibie. Despite Habibie's efforts to distance himself from Suharto's regime and to appear as democratically reformist as possible, the mood remained volatile as of late 1998.

DISCUSSION

The conventional view among economists and many political scientists is that reforms of the type that economies in East Asia (and, before them, in Latin America and elsewhere) were called on to undertake require insulated, autonomous executives who can act speedily and decisively. In other words, democracy, even when not hostile to reform, complicates it. The systematic evidence from the 1970s and 1980s, as well as the more recent Asian experience, suggests that the opposite is closer to the truth.[10]

The sweeping market-oriented reforms that Latin American countries undertook during the last decade were the product mostly of democratic governments. This has prompted scholars of the region to reevaluate the relationship between democratic politics and economic management, finding much more good in democracy than was indicated in the earlier literature (Dominguez 1998; Hagopian 1998). The experience of the former socialist economies has been similar, suggesting that democratization may be a complement to speedy stabilization and reform

(Aslund, Boone, and Johnson, 1996). An interesting paper by Hellman (1998) concludes: "Postcommunist systems with a higher level of political participation and competition [e.g. Poland and the Czech Republic] have been able to adopt and maintain more comprehensive economic reforms than states largely insulated from mass politics and electoral pressure [e.g. Ukraine and Belarus]" (pp. 233-234). In Hellman's view, political systems where power is concentrated allow "winners" to stop reform in its tracks so as to keep access to the rents that partial reforms create. Broader political participation and competition acts as a counterweight to this tendency.[11]

In his 1861 book *Representative Government,* John Stuart Mill described the advantages of the democratic form of government (in comparison to dictatorships) in terms that remain highly relevant. One of the special merits of democratic participation in public affairs, he wrote, is that it makes the citizen more willing to see others' points of view, to compromise, and to cooperate. The citizen

is called upon, while so engaged, to weigh interests not his own; to be guided, in case of conflicting claims, by another rule than his private partialities; to apply, at every turn, principles and maxims which have for their reason of existence the common good: and he usually finds associated with him in the same work minds more familiarised than his own with these ideas and operations, whose study it will be to supply reasons to his understanding, and stimulation to his feeling for the general interest. He is made to feel himself one of the public, and whatever is for their benefit to be for his benefit. Where this school of public spirit does not exist, scarcely any sense is entertained that private persons, in no eminent social situation, owe any duties to society, except to obey the laws and submit to the government. There is no unselfish sentiment of identification with the public. Every thought or feeling, either of interest or of duty, is absorbed in the individual and in the family. The man never thinks of any collective interest, of any objects to be pursued jointly with others, but only in competition with them, and in some measure at their expense. A neighbour, not being an ally or an associate, since he is never engaged in any common undertaking for joint benefit, is therefore only a rival. Thus even private morality suffers, while public is actually extinct.[12]

The passage encapsulates well the contrasting ways in which the citizenry reacted to the exigencies of adjustment in Indonesia on the one hand, and in Thailand and South Korea on the other.[13]

IMPROVING THE INSTITUTIONS
OF CONFLICT MANAGEMENT

■ THE WORLD MARKET IS A SOURCE OF DISRUPTION and upheaval as much as it is an opportunity for profit and economic growth. Without the complementary institutions at home—in the areas of governance, judiciary, civil and political liberties, social insurance, and education—one gets too much of the former and too little of the latter. The weakness of the domestic institutions of conflict management was the Achilles' heel of the development strategy pursued in Latin America, the Middle East, and elsewhere, and this is what made countries in these regions so susceptible to the external shocks of the 1970s.

This weakness persists. Reforms in the areas of macroeconomic policy, trade policy, deregulation, and privatization have not been matched by deeper reforms of political institutions, bureaucracies, judiciaries, and social safety nets. As Dominguez (1997, pp. 106-112) argues with reference to Latin America:

> Popular democratic representation requires a well-organized and articulate labor movement, capable of functioning in a market economy and standing up for the rights of workers. Democratic politics requires contestation between organized forces; democracy would be wounded if there were no appropriate counterparts to business power.... Though the reasons vary, the role of parliaments and the quality of executive-legislative relations still widely fail to foster the consolidation of democracy.... Compared to the national legislatures of Brazil, Ecuador, Colombia, and Honduras, the U.S. Congress is a model of democratic responsiveness, party discipline, member responsibility, policy attention, and coherence. [In Brazil and Ecuador,] as many as a third of the legislators cross the aisle during one term of office . . . Presidentialism—rule by decree—is the natural offspring of such practices . . . The turn towards the market [in Latin America] has also coincided with spectacular cases of corruption that led to the impeachments of presidents Collor in Brazil and Perez in Venezuela . . . .

And, of course, the discrediting of Salinas in Mexico.

Meanwhile, the world economy has hardly become a safer place—ask the Thai or the Indonesians if you have any doubt. This leaves developing countries highly vulnerable. Without an internal strategy of institutional reform to complement the external strategy of opening up, they risk vulnerability to the kinds of protracted crises from which many of them have begun to recover only recently.

There are at least three components of such an institutional reform strategy: improving the credibility of the state apparatus, improving mechanisms of voice, and improving social safety nets and social insurance.

IMPROVING THE CREDIBILITY OF THE STATE APPARATUS

There has been much progress on the macroeconomic policy front in some countries, especially in Latin America. But now this credibility has to be extended beyond the macroeconomic field. There is a great need to improve the quality of the judiciary and of the public bureaucracy, and to root out corruption. The state cannot play the role of honest broker in mediating social conflict—as it does so often in East Asia—if it is not perceived as trustworthy and competent.

IMPROVING MECHANISMS OF VOICE

There is a need to improve the channels through which nonelites (indigenous peoples, workers, and farmers) can make themselves heard and to bring them (or their representatives) into the decision-making councils. The top-down, technocratic style that is well suited to macroeconomic stabilization is not well suited to the challenges of the second stage of reform. These later reforms will not achieve popular legitimacy unless they are perceived to be the result of a broader deliberation at the national level. Looked at from this perspective, a strong, widely based trade union movement is a good thing, not a bad thing. Having strong, disciplined political parties is a good thing, not a bad thing. A strong executive is also good, but even better when it uses its autonomy to reach out and strike bargains and alliances with the popular sectors.

It has now become commonplace to point out that market-oriented reforms require social safety nets to prevent individuals from falling through the cracks as economic change unfolds. Social safety nets are in fact part and parcel of modern capitalism, and an important reason for its endurance. As Jacoby (1998, p. 1) emphasizes, "over the last one hundred years, modern societies have developed a diverse set of institutions for pooling labor-market risk and indemnifying against it."

Yet it is not sufficiently appreciated what an important role social insurance has played in those countries that were most successful in integrating themselves into the world economy in the postwar period (or reintegrating themselves, as in the case of Western Europe). In Western Europe, the idea of providing social protection in order to insulate and cushion broad segments of society from market risks—particularly those risks of external origin—was (and to some extent remains) an ingrained habit. This is evident in the welfare state that has grown during the postwar era and in the huge growth in income transfers. It is only a mild exaggeration to say that the European welfare state is the flip side of the open economy (Rodrik 1997b). In East Asia, the same function has been performed not by social programs and income transfers but by a combination of enterprise policies (such as lifetime employment and the provision of social services), extensive product and labor market regulations (which slowed down the pace of change), and a much more gradual, controlled type of external liberalization.

As is now evident, the approaches in Europe and East Asia have their problems. However, it is clear that the provision of social insurance is an *important component* of market reforms—it cushions the blow of liberalization among those most severely affected, it helps maintain the legitimacy of these reforms, and it averts backlashes against the distributional and social consequences of integration into the world economy.

There is no how-to manual for designing the appropriate institutions of conflict management, especially where the representation of "voice" is concerned. The issues are complex, and it is a fair bet that we will need a considerable amount of institutional innovation and experimentation before we develop strong intuitions about the kinds of mechanism that have to develop. From the perspective of this chapter, however, the key is to recognize that institutions of conflict management are a necessary complement to openness.

In the absence of such institutions, openness is likely to foster domestic social conflicts that will prove damaging not only in their own right, but will be also detrimental to economic growth in the long run.

. . . .

CONCLUSION

■   I HAVE ARGUED THAT THE DEVELOPMENT COMMUNITY has internalized the wrong lessons from the experience of countries in Latin America and elsewhere that adopted the ISI strategy. The correct interpretation of this experience goes something like this:

■ First, ISI worked rather well for about two decades. It brought unprecedented economic growth to scores of countries in Latin America, the Middle East, and North Africa, and even to some in Sub-Saharan Africa.

■ Second, when the economies of these same countries began to fall apart in the second half of the 1970s, the reasons had little to do with ISI policies per se or the extent of government interventions in the microeconomic sphere. Countries that weathered the storm were those in which governments undertook the appropriate *macro*economic adjustments (in the areas of fiscal, monetary, and exchange-rate policy) rapidly and decisively.

■ Third, and more fundamentally, success in adopting these macroeconomic adjustments was linked to deeper social determinants. It was the ability to manage the domestic social conflicts triggered by the turbulence of the world economy during the 1970s that made the difference between continued growth and economic collapse. Countries with deeper social divisions and weaker institutions of conflict management experienced greater economic deterioration in response to the external shocks of the 1970s.

Taken together, these points provide an interpretation of recent economic history that is at odds with much current thinking. By emphasizing the importance of social conflicts and institutions—at the expense of trade strategy and industrial policies—they also suggest quite a different perspective on development policy. If I am right, the main difference between Latin America, say, and East Asia was not that the former remained closed and isolated while the latter integrated itself with the world economy. The main difference was that

Latin America did a much worse job of dealing with the turbulence generated by the world economy. The countries that got into trouble were those that could not manage openness, not those that were insufficiently open.

Hence, improving the quality of institutions of conflict management is a critical complement to openness. These institutions help adjudicate distributional contests within a framework of rules and accepted procedures— that is, without open conflict and hostilities. Democratic institutions, an independent and effective judiciary, an honest bureaucracy, and institution-alized modes of social insurance are among the most significant of conflict-management institutions. I have shown in this chapter how such institutions have had demonstrable benefits—and in the case of countries lacking them, severe adverse effects—in terms of economic performance subsequent to the shocks of the 1970s.

The recent Asian crisis provides further support for this perspec-tive, and once again highlights the important role played by institutions of conflict management. In South Korea and Thailand, where new democratic institutions provide for mechanisms of voice and contestation, political sys-tems have turned out to be better—at least so far—at delivering adjust-ment policies than in Indonesia, where a personal dictatorship proved to be the recipe for a descent into chaos.

Conflict management institutions play a far more important role in generating the capacity to handle external turbulence than conventional eco-nomic analysis has generally allowed. The evidence reveals a certain num-ber of "stylized facts" regarding which types of social and political arrangements work better than others, but clearly we need to learn a lot more. More research, particularly of a cross-disciplinary kind, is needed to sharpen understanding of these links.

NOTES

[1] Sub-Saharan African countries were disproportionately represented in this group, bringing down the region's average. The list of 10 includes Niger, Sudan, Chad, Bangladesh, Somalia, Rwanda, Haiti, Senegal, Madagascar, and Nepal. Note, moreover, that growth rates of GDP can be misleading indicators of increases in well-being if they are calculated at distorted domes-tic prices, which diverge from "shadow" prices. However, growth data from the Penn World Tables, calculated using international prices, are less susceptible to this problem and yield quite similar results. I use World Bank data here because these data cover a more recent period.

[2] These figures come from the World Bank's *World Data 1995* CD-ROM.

[3] For an interesting political explanation, motivated by the Argentinean experience, for why many countries chose ISI policies, see Robinson (1997). Robinson argues that in resource-rich

countries such as Argentina, open trade policies would have shifted power to agricultural interests, and were therefore blocked by capitalists.

[4] One explanation for Argentina's dismal performance prior to 1973 is that the kind of social conflicts that were exacerbated by the shocks of the 1970s in other countries (see discussion below) appeared much earlier in Argentina, with adverse effects on the quality of policymaking. The deep cleavage between rural and urban interests in Argentina fostered wide swings in policy as well as highly restrictive trade policies (see O'Donnell 1979). I am grateful to James A. Robinson for the pointers on the Argentinean case and the reference to O'Donnell.

[5] The "discovery" during the Asian financial crisis that began in 1997 that not all investment projects in the world's most outward-oriented countries were models of efficiency is also relevant here. Standard cost-benefit analysis, unable to pinpoint positive externalities with any degree of certainty, is likely to pass a negative judgment on key investments not only in fast-growing developing countries but in some early industrializers such as the United States.

[6] For a more balanced appraisal of ISI than is common these days, see Bruton (1998).

[7] For a parallel argument stressing macroeconomic mismanagement and debt crises, and de-emphasizing the role of trade orientation, see Cohen (1997).

[8] This point is disputed by many, and goes against the official view of the IMF (Fischer 1998). The argument that "structural" aspects of the East Asian model were not at the root of the crisis is well put by Stiglitz (1998) and Radelet and Sachs (1998). This is not to say that these economies did not have structural weaknesses, in particular an over-reliance on governmental steering of the economy that had probably outlived its usefulness. But as Stiglitz points out, financial crises break out with some regularity in economies ranging from Scandinavia to the United States, regardless of form of economic management and standards of transparency.

[9] South Korea was not a democracy in 1980, and its relatively smooth adjustment at the time (recall the comparison with Brazil and Turkey) may call into question the emphasis I place on the importance of democratic institutions in 1997. But South Korea had a number of important advantages along other dimensions I have also stressed: a high-quality bureaucracy, a high degree of rule of law, relatively limited income inequality, and virtually no ethnic or linguistic cleavages.

[10] The voluminous empirical literature on the long-run consequences of political democracy for economic growth has generally yielded ambiguous results (Bhalla forthcoming; Przeworski and Limongi 1993; Helliwell 1994; Barro 1996). However, more recent studies show that democracies produce a better balance between risk and reward: that is, the level of aggregate economic instability tends to be much lower under democracies. See Rodrik (1997d), Chandra (1998), and Quinn and Woolley (1998). The latter set of findings is consistent with the systematic evidence presented earlier on the superior performance of democracies when confronted with external shocks, as well as with the recent evidence from East Asia.

[11] There is also some recent econometric evidence suggesting that public investment projects yield higher economic returns in environments with greater civil liberties and democracy (Pritchett and Kaufmann 1998).

[12] From Chapter 3 of Mill (1861), taken from http://english-www.hss.cmu.edu/Philosophy/mill-representative-govt.txt. I owe the reference to this passage to Bell (1998).

[13] One can reinterpret Mill's discussion also in terms of *social capital*, a term that is currently much in vogue. Mill's argument is that democracy promotes greater social capital—the capacity to undertake projects for the collective good—by establishing connections among individuals and binding them into civil society. For a recent paper that provides some evidence on "social capabilities" and social capital in fostering growth, see Temple and Johnson (1998).

Chapter 5
Is Africa
Different?

INTRODUCTION

■ THE ANSWER TO THE QUESTION POSED by this chapter's title, I will argue, is no. To be sure, Sub-Saharan Africa is poorer than any other region in the world, and many of its economies have declined much more precipitously than others elsewhere. The region faces much greater public-health challenges, and it suffers from severe climactic and geographical disadvantages. But the basic lessons for economic policy I have discussed in the preceding chapters apply equally well to the African countries. Because most of the African economies are small, they cannot afford to close themselves off from the world economy—perhaps more than any other region, Africa needs imports of capital goods, intermediate inputs, and ideas. At the same time, it is important to realize that openness is no panacea, and that it has to be complemented with domestic investment and better institutions of conflict management if sustainable economic growth is to result.

I argue in this chapter that trade policy in Sub-Saharan Africa works in much the same way that it does elsewhere.[1] High levels of trade restrictions (as well as overvalued currencies) have seriously discouraged exports in the past, and their reduction can be expected to result in significantly improved trade performance in the region. Removal of export restrictions, dismantling of marketing boards, relaxation of quantitative restrictions on imports, and lowering of import tariffs will sharply increase traditional and nontraditional exports. There is little reason for pessimism in this respect, or for concern that Africa's different conditions—its poor infrastructure, its geography, or its dependence on a limited number of primary products—make it a special case in which exports are not responsive to prices or to the traditional instruments of commercial policy.

Although trade reforms are a potent means of boosting trade volumes, the evidence suggests that their influence on economic growth is generally much weaker. As I have argued earlier in this book, an increase in the share of national income that is exported does not in itself generate growth in per capita income. This is as true in Africa as it is elsewhere. Over the 1964-1994 period, there were five countries in Africa that increased the dollar value of their exports of manufactures to the countries of the OECD at an annual average rate of 20 percent or more: Mauritius, Mali, Burkina Faso, Côte d'Ivoire, and Niger. Only the first of these countries is an unqualified success story.

The fundamentals for long-term growth are investments in physical capital and human resources. These are, in turn, made possible by physical infrastructure, macroeconomic stability, the rule of law, and solid institutions. Governments that focus their efforts on these areas will be rewarded with increased rates of economic growth.

The role of trade policy in economic growth in Africa is largely auxiliary and of an enabling nature: extremes of export taxation and import restrictions can surely suffocate nascent economic activity, but an open trade regime on its own will not set an economy on a sustained growth path. Too much focus on "outward orientation" and "openness" can even be counterproductive if it diverts policymakers' attention from the growth fundamentals and results in the treatment of trade, rather than per capita income, as a yardstick of success.

. . . .

AN OVERVIEW OF AFRICAN ECONOMIC PERFORMANCE

■   SINCE THE MID-1990S, VARIOUS AFRICAN ECONOMIES have enjoyed some of the highest growth rates experienced in the region in at least a decade. Along with a wave of political change and democratization, this performance has generated a degree of optimism about Africa's future, raising hopes that the region's 600 million people can be eventually lifted out of poverty and destitution. But optimism must be tempered by the understanding that the countries with the fastest growing economies in Sub-Saharan Africa have only begun to recover from debilitating civil wars or long periods of economic decline. For many of them, it will require growth at East Asian rates for the better part of a decade *just* to make up for lost ground. There are at least 10 countries in the region where GDP per capita is lower now than in 1960.[2] Uganda and Ghana, the two most aggressive reformers, have yet to regain their 1970 level of per capita GDP despite substantial growth since the mid-1980s.

However, the rate of economic growth has not been dismal in all countries of the region. Over the entire 1960-1994 period, three countries experienced growth of three percent or more in real per capita GDP per annum (Botswana, Lesotho, and Mauritius), and at least three more

TABLE 5.1. PER CAPITA GDP GROWTH RATES IN SUB-SAHARAN AFRICA
(percent)

Country	1960-1994	1960-1973	1973-1984	1984-1994
Benin	0.10	0.29	0.16	-0.22
Botswana	5.94	6.15	7.34	4.11
Burkina Faso	n.a.	n.a.	1.75	0.53
Burundi	1.26	2.95	0.86	-0.51
Cameroon	0.53	0.97	4.68	-4.62
Cape Verde	n.a.	n.a.	6.32	2.45
Central African Republic	-0.60	0.26	-0.81	-1.49
Chad	-0.61	-1.75	-1.17	1.48
Comoros	n.a.	n.a.	n.a.	-1.39
Congo	1.72	2.46	5.75	-3.69
Côte d'Ivoire	0.95	5.63	-0.20	-3.88
Ethiopia	n.a.	n.a.	n.a.	-0.38
Gabon	0.71	4.72	0.43	-4.20
Gambia	1.09	2.80	1.27	-1.33
Ghana	-0.55	0.03	-2.96	1.34
Guinea-Bissau	n.a.	n.a.	-1.41	2.13
Kenya	1.54	3.40	0.25	0.54
Lesotho	3.57	4.94	1.75	3.80
Liberia	n.a.	1.28	-2.53	n.a.
Madagascar	-1.54	-0.33	-2.63	-1.91
Malawi	0.76	2.85	0.78	-1.98
Mali	0.39	0.32	0.11	0.80
Mauritania	0.93	2.85	-0.83	0.38
Mauritius	3.24	3.14	0.96	5.22
Mozambique	n.a.	n.a.	n.a.	3.96
Namibia	n.a.	n.a.	n.a.	0.31
Niger	-1.87	-2.00	-1.85	-1.74
Nigeria	0.14	1.27	-2.53	1.62
Rwanda	-2.35	-0.77	2.08	-9.29
São Tomé and Principe	n.a.	n.a.	0.33	-0.45
Senegal	-0.44	-0.44	-0.22	-0.67
Seychelles	2.98	2.67	2.34	4.09
Sierra Leone	n.a.	n.a.	0.98	-3.20
Somalia	n.a.	-0.95	-0.12	n.a.
South Africa	0.50	2.39	0.19	-1.62
Sudan	-0.18	-1.79	1.76	-0.23
Swaziland	2.67	6.74	0.14	0.16
Tanzania	-0.03	2.64	-3.65	0.50
Togo	0.69	4.17	-0.60	-2.42
Uganda	n.a.	n.a.	n.a.	1.40
Zaire	n.a.	n.a.	-3.24	n.a.
Zambia	-1.36	0.63	-2.85	-2.32
Zimbabwe	0.75	2.58	-0.85	0.16
Average	**0.70**	**1.88**	**0.31**	**-0.31**

Source: World Bank data.

surpassed two percent (Seychelles and Swaziland; see Table 5.1). Many others have experienced high growth over a period of a decade or more: Côte d'Ivoire, Gabon, Kenya, and Togo during 1960-1973, and Congo and Cameroon during 1973-1984, for example. An important message that comes out of Table 5.1 is that African countries *are* able to grow at satisfactory rates over extended periods when the circumstances are right. This is a useful message as it allows us to be optimistic about the prospects for the region.

As in other regions, investment has made a big difference to economic performance over the long run. Investment rates in Africa have tended to be low by international standards. At international prices, the average investment rate in Sub-Saharan Africa over the 1960-1989 period was 11 percent of GDP, which is half the rate for East Asia (22 percent) and well below the rate for Latin America (17 percent).[3] Focusing on African countries alone, one sees differences in investment rates that have been perhaps the most important determinant of variation in long-term growth rates. As Figure 5.1 shows, there is a tight relationship between investment/GDP ratios in individual countries and per capita growth rates over 1960-1994. Countries whose economies have grown fast, such as Botswana and Mauritius, have had much higher investment rates than laggards such as Rwanda, Madagascar, and Niger. Although some countries' economies have grown less rapidly than what their investment rates would indicate (e.g., Zambia), these are the exceptions, not the rule.

As the previous set of figures showed, Africa has experienced enormous instability in economic performance. To cite one important example, Côte d'Ivoire has been transformed from one of the miracle economies of Africa during 1960-1973 (with a growth rate in per capita income of 5.6 percent) to a basket case during 1984-1994 (with a growth rate of -3.9 percent). Resource booms and cycles in commodity prices account for some, but not all, of these ups and downs. As I argued in the previous chapter, the inability to respond to these cycles with appropriate macroeconomic policies has magnified the economic consequences of external volatility. In Côte d'Ivoire's case, for example, the fixed exchange rate of the CFA (Communauté Financière Africaine) franc proved to be a disaster once coffee and cocoa prices collapsed.

More fundamentally, the maintenance of macroeconomic stability in Africa has been hampered by weak institutions of conflict management. In this sense, the African experience is qualitatively no different from that of the other regions on which I focused in the previous chapter, except insofar as ethnic divisions are generally a more serious problem in Africa. The weakness of public institutions and in governance styles has made Africa an excessively risky environment for economic activity (Collier 1995), which has had a depressant effect on private investment levels.

African countries with relatively greater civil liberties and political rights have had higher-quality institutions and have been more adept at dealing with economic shocks. This is shown in Figure 5.2, which is reminiscent of Figures 4.5 and 4.6 in the previous chapter but is restricted to a sample of Sub-Saharan African countries.[4] Although most African countries were autocracies until recently, those among them with more democratic institutions—Mauritius, Botswana, and Seychelles—have adjusted to terms-of-

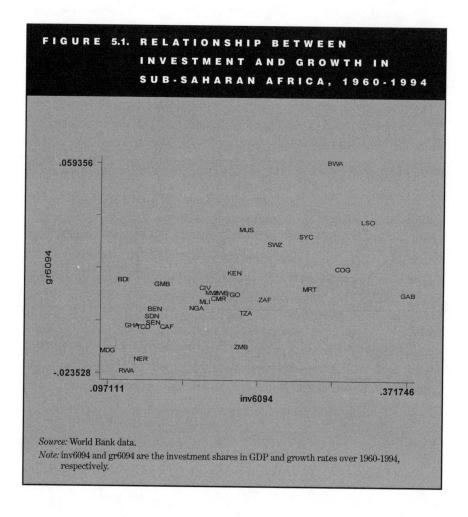

FIGURE 5.1. RELATIONSHIP BETWEEN INVESTMENT AND GROWTH IN SUB-SAHARAN AFRICA, 1960-1994

Source: World Bank data.

Note: inv6094 and gr6094 are the investment shares in GDP and growth rates over 1960-1994, respectively.

trade shocks and other external disturbances much better. Mauritius is a particularly significant example, as it is a society with deep ethnic divisions (the contending groups including Creoles, Indians, and Franco-Mauritians, among others), and one that was perceived to face very poor economic prospects when independence was achieved in 1968. Democracy has enabled major Mauritian social actors (including ethnic groups) to be drawn into decision-making councils and has produced relatively generous social policies that maintain social peace despite a turbulent history.[5]

These pieces of evidence give reason to believe that the democratic transitions in Africa may eventually prove to be a boon on economic grounds as well. As Barkan and Gordon (1998) emphasize, the two countries with the

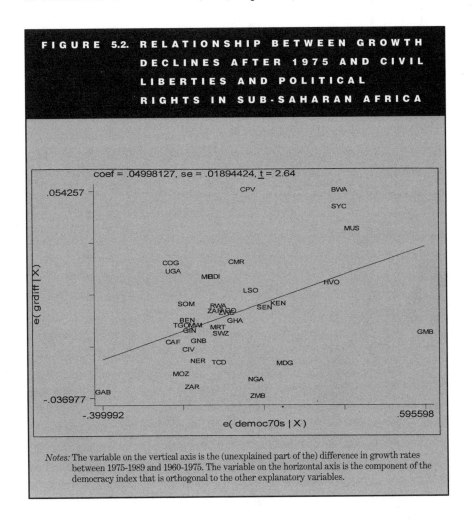

FIGURE 5.2. RELATIONSHIP BETWEEN GROWTH DECLINES AFTER 1975 AND CIVIL LIBERTIES AND POLITICAL RIGHTS IN SUB-SAHARAN AFRICA

Notes: The variable on the vertical axis is the (unexplained part of the) difference in growth rates between 1975-1989 and 1960-1975. The variable on the horizontal axis is the component of the democracy index that is orthogonal to the other explanatory variables.

best long-term growth records in Africa are the ones with the longest records of democratic rule, Botswana and Mauritius. Growth has recently returned to Benin, Ghana, Mozambique, and South Africa, countries where democratization has gone farthest. As Barkan and Gordon say, "The clear lesson from Africa is that economic renewal and democratization go hand in hand" (p. 108).[6]

. . . .

WHY IS AFRICA "MARGINALIZED" IN WORLD TRADE?

■ TRADE BARRIERS IN SUB-SAHARAN AFRICA have been generally high, and they have come down only slowly, and with much equivocation. Comparative evidence on regional trade barriers is presented in Chapter 1. This evidence shows that until the early 1990s, trade restrictions in Africa were comparable in magnitude to those prevailing in Latin America. But, as Tables 1.2 and 1.3 also show, the region's policymakers have displayed much less enthusiasm for the kind of sweeping trade reforms that have recently been enacted in Latin American economies—as well as in most of the former socialist economies of Eastern Europe and Central Asia. While tariff and nontariff barriers have come down, and currencies have depreciated, the level of trade restrictions remains higher in Sub-Saharan Africa than in any other region. Most African countries chose not to take advantage of the Uruguay Round to bind their tariffs at low levels. Tariffs were typically bound at levels far exceeding current levels, and often at levels exceeding 100 percent (Harrold 1995).

Sub-Saharan Africa's trade has grown slowly since the 1950s, with the result that the region's share of world trade stands today around one percent, down from more than three percent in the mid-1950s (Yeats 1997, p. 1). However, Africa's marginalization in world trade is primarily due to the continent's lagging performance in terms of output growth. It does not result from trade ratios (relative to GDP) that have declined or are low by cross-national standards. As I show below, African countries trade on average as much as would be expected by international norms once their income levels and the size of their economies are taken into account. It is because they have failed to expand their economies at sufficient rates that their importance in world trade has shrunk. Consequently, the way to reverse the trend is not to target the region's trade volumes per se, but to raise overall growth rates.

Figure 5.3 shows the trends in export/GDP ratios since 1960 by regional groupings. At constant relative prices, this ratio has remained more or less stable in Sub-Saharan Africa in a range between 26 and 30 percent, and, if anything, it has increased since the early 1980s. The figure makes clear that the region is not an outlier in terms of the trends observed in other regions. East Asia's export ratio has increased the most, but even in this case, the phenomenal rise in that region's importance in world trade is clearly due to its very rapid output growth rather than the increase in its export/GDP ratio.

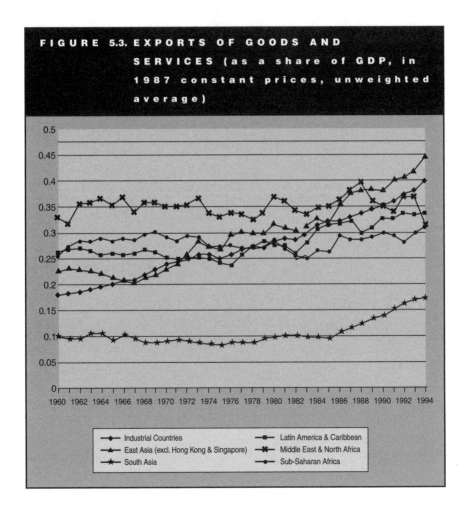

FIGURE 5.3. EXPORTS OF GOODS AND SERVICES (as a share of GDP, in 1987 constant prices, unweighted average)

Table 5.2 shows the results from cross-national regressions where I use a large sample of countries to relate the observed shares of exports in GDP to levels of national income per capita and to country size.[7] In each case, I include a dummy variable for Sub-Saharan Africa (as well as other country groupings) to check whether the estimated coefficient is negative and statistically significant, as it would be if the region were an underperformer.

TABLE 5.2. DOES AFRICA TRADE TOO LITTLE?

	Dependent variable: ratio of exports to GDP, 1990-94		
	(1)	(2)	(3)
Sub-Saharan Africa	0.10	0.06	-0.02
	(0.07)	(0.09)	(0.03)
East Asia	0.49*	0.47*	0.46**
	(0.08)	(0.14)	(0.18)
Latin America	0.04	0.03	(0.03)
	(0.06)	(0.06)	(0.04)
In per capita income	0.10*	0.09**	
	(0.03)	(0.03)	
In population	-0.04**	-0.05***	
	(0.02)	(0.03)	
In land area	-0.06*	-0.06**	
	(0.01)	(0.03)	
In distance		0.002	
		(0.062)	
"Gravity" component of openness[a]			0.44*
			(0.14)
Constant	0.50	0.68	0.20*
	(0.38)	(0.58)	(0.03)
R^2	0.63	0.62	0.49
N	100	80	108

Notes: [a]Based on Frankel and Romer (1996).
Heteroskedasticity-consistent standard errors are in parentheses.
Levels of significance: * 99 percent; ** 95 percent; *** 90 percent.

The regression in column 1 shows that country size (as measured by population and land area) and per capita income are very strong determinants of the openness of an economy. Smaller and richer countries trade more (as a share of their GDP). The estimated coefficients imply that a doubling of per capita income increases exports by 10 percent of GDP, while doubling country size decreases them by four to six percent. In column 2, I have added as a regressor a measure of geographical distance from the world's leading traders (taken from Barro and Lee 1994). This variable enters with an insignificant coefficient, and its presence makes little difference to the estimated coefficients on the other regressors. Finally, in column 3, I include a measure of the gravity component of trade, drawn from the work of Frankel and Romer (1996), who have estimated the expected volume of trade for a large sample of countries based purely on geographical determinants.

In none of these regressions is the estimated coefficient on the dummy variable for Sub-Saharan Africa statistically significant. Once size and per capita income are controlled, African countries on the whole do not appear to be outliers. In the first two regressions, the estimated coefficient is actually positive (indicating that, if anything, Africa exports more than is expected on the basis of income levels and size). In the third regression, the coefficient turns negative but is very small (and insignificant). The bottom line is this: Africa trades *on average* as much as is to be expected given its geography and its level of per capita income.[8] A recent, more extensive study by Coe and Hoffmaister (1998), based on bilateral trade flows and using a wider range of geographical controls, has reached the same conclusion.[9]

Therefore, the marginalization of Africa in world trade is the consequence of two factors: first, Africa's GDP per capita has grown more slowly than other regions'; and second, the elasticity of trade with respect to output exceeds unity. As other countries have grown, their trade volumes have expanded more than proportionately. Taking the region as a whole, there is little evidence that trade policies have repressed trade volumes below cross-national benchmarks, unless they have done so indirectly through their depressing effect on incomes.[10] The encouraging message is that the answer to Africa's trade woes is the same as the answer to its broader economic difficulties: a rise in per capita income. Once the focus is shifted from trade to economic growth in general, we are forced to think more broadly about the whole range of growth determinants, and not just about impediments to exchanges at the border.

WHAT DETERMINES TRADE
PERFORMANCE IN AFRICA?

■   AVERAGES FOR SUB-SAHARAN AFRICAN TRADE performance hide tremendous variation across countries. As is true with growth, there are many examples of good performance alongside the better- known cases of dismal failure. How much of the variation in trade performance within Africa is due to differences in exogenous and uncontrollable factors such as geography and the external terms of trade, and how much to differences in domestic policies? The evidence suggests that geography and trade policy both play an important role, with the terms of trade having no perceptible impact.

These conclusions come out of a set of regressions based on pooled cross-section, time-series data. I have split the 1964-1994 period into three subperiods (1964-1974, 1975-1984, and 1985-1994) to provide up to three observations per country. The dependent variables are the shares of trade in GDP (either total trade or exports) and their rate of growth. These are regressed on a range of determinants, including trade policies, income levels, and geographic variables. The sample consists of 37 Sub-Saharan African countries.[11]

Table 5.3 shows the first set of results on trade shares. The dependent variable here is either the sum of exports and imports as a share of GDP ($(x+m)/y$) or just the share of exports (x/y). As regressors, I include the following in addition to trade policy indicators: the logs of (initial) per capita income and population, a dummy for land-locked countries (*access*), and a measure of the proportion of a country's land area that is subject to a tropical climate (*tropics*). The last two variables are taken from Sachs and Warner (1997). The estimated coefficients on these regressors confirm that trade volumes (in relation to national output) tend to rise with level of income and fall with population. Being landlocked and in the tropics depresses trade.[12]

The regressions indicate that trade restrictions also make a significant difference. I calculated the ad valorem equivalent of international trade taxes by dividing tax revenue from all border taxes by the volume of total trade. Obviously, this indicator has shortcomings as a measure of the restrictiveness of trade policies. It underestimates the effects of extremely high taxes that bring in little revenue, ignores nontariff barriers and the role of

TABLE 5.3. DETERMINANTS OF TRADE VOLUMES IN SUB-SAHARAN AFRICA

	Dependent variable									
	(x+m)/y					x/y			(x+m)/y	x/y
	(1)	(2)	(3)	(4)	(5)	(6)	(7)	(8)	(9)	(10)
Taxes on trade	-1.99* (0.37)		-2.11* (0.40)		-1.97* (0.44)	-1.20* (0.23)			-0.93 (0.74)	-0.84** (0.35)
Import taxes		-0.82* (0.31)		-1.37* (0.38)			-0.39** (0.21)	-0.85* (0.22)		
Export taxes		-1.10* (0.22)		-0.86* (0.26)			-0.52* (0.12)	-0.34** (0.14)		
Black market premium			-0.02** (0.01)	-0.03** (0.01)	-0.03* (0.01)			-0.01*** (0.01)		
Nontariff barriers					-0.08 (0.07)			-0.05 (0.04)		
Log per capita income	0.11* (0.04)	0.12* (0.04)	0.10** (0.04)	0.12* (0.04)	0.14* (0.05)	0.13* (0.03)	0.14* (0.03)	0.13* (0.03)	0.13*** (0.08)	0.10* (0.04)
Log population	-0.11* (0.19)	-0.11* (0.02)	-0.11* (0.02)	-0.11* (0.02)	-0.09* (0.02)	-0.04* (0.01)	-0.04* (0.01)	-0.02*** (0.01)		
Access	-0.05 (0.04)	-0.03 (0.04)	-0.07*** (0.04)	-0.07*** (0.04)	-0.01 (0.04)	0.002 (0.02)	0.01 (0.03)	0.02 (0.03)		
Tropics	-0.58* (0.09)	-0.50* (0.09)	-0.62* (0.10)	-0.57* (0.10)	1.44* (0.42)	-0.08 (0.07)	-0.04 (0.08)	0.61** (0.29)		
Country dummies	no	no	no	no	no	no	no	no	yes	yes
N	92	91	83	82	54	92	91	54	93	93
R²	0.78	0.79	0.81	0.81	0.74	0.67	0.63	0.73	0.34	0.55
Root MSE	0.16	0.16	0.15	0.16	0.13	0.10	0.11	0.07		

Notes: Regressions are performed on pooled data covering period averages for 1964-1974, 1975-1984, and 1985-1994. All regressions include dummies for each of the periods (coefficients not shown). Robust standard errors are reported in parenthesis. Levels of statistical significance are as follows:
 *99% level
 **95% level
 ***90% level

implicit export taxation through commodity boards, and overlooks the role of smuggling.[13] But the indicator has the advantage of being available for a large number of African countries. In addition, it is one of the few trade policy measures for which a consistent time series can be constructed for most African countries, allowing us to exploit the time-series dimension in the data.

This measure of trade taxation correlates very strongly, and negatively, with trade performance. Moreover, import taxes and export taxes enter individually with statistically significant coefficients. The magnitude of the estimated coefficients on import and export taxes, respectively, are generally statistically indistinguishable from each other, regardless of whether *exports* or *total trade* is used as the dependent variable. This is a remarkable confirmation of the Lerner symmetry theorem, which says that import taxes are equivalent to export taxes, and vice versa, in all respects.[14] The estimated coefficients suggest that a reduction in import or export taxes of 10 percentage points boosts exports by about five percentage points of GDP. A visual sense of the impact is provided in Figure 5.4, which shows a partial scatter plot relating export shares to trade taxes. I also find that black-market premiums enter with negative and statistically significant coefficients.

The last two columns of Table 5.3 show the results when a full set of country fixed effects are included. (Period effects are included in all of the regressions.) The coefficient on trade taxes remains negative and large, and is either significant or borderline significant in the case of the export equations. This is striking in view of the fact that with a full set of country dummies, the effect of trade taxes on exports is identified purely from the time-series variation *within* each country, which in this case is limited to a maximum of three observations.

The R^2s are in the range of 0.63 to 0.81, indicating that a relatively small number of variables (country size, per capita income, geography, and taxation of trade) account well for the variation in trade shares in the region. I have tried a number of additional explanatory variables, but the results remain largely unaltered. In particular, I experimented with the external terms of trade and found that neither the growth rate of the terms of trade over this period nor its volatility enters the regression with anything approaching statistical significance.

In Table 5.4, I check how well the same set of explanatory variables does in explaining *growth* of trade over the 1964-1994 period. The dependent variable in these regressions is the average growth rate of the trade

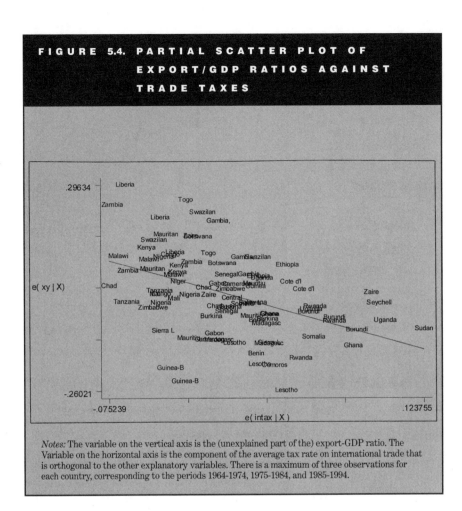

FIGURE 5.4. PARTIAL SCATTER PLOT OF EXPORT/GDP RATIOS AGAINST TRADE TAXES

Notes: The variable on the vertical axis is the (unexplained part of the) export-GDP ratio. The Variable on the horizontal axis is the component of the average tax rate on international trade that is orthogonal to the other explanatory variables. There is a maximum of three observations for each country, corresponding to the periods 1964-1974, 1975-1984, and 1985-1994.

shares used in Table 5.3. The fit of these regressions is significantly worse, with R²s ranging from 0.08 to 0.29. This is mainly due to the fact that the exogenous variables (initial per capita income, country size, and geography) do not seem to play a significant role in determining changes in the volume of trade. However, there is evidence that trade taxes and black-market premiums both have significant depressing effects on export growth. According to the results in column 2, a 10 percent increase in taxes on all trade is associated with a reduction in export growth (as a share of GDP) of three percent per annum. Strikingly, trade taxes remain a statistically significant determinant of trade growth even after a full set of country fixed

TABLE 5.4. DETERMINANTS OF GROWTH OF TRADE IN SUB-SAHARAN AFRICA

| | Dependent variable: growth of | | | | | |
| | (x+m)/y | x/y | | | | (x+m)/y |
	(1)	(2)	(3)	(4)	(5)	(6)
Taxes on trade	-0.14	-0.32*	-0.28**	-0.33**	-0.72*	
	(0.11)	(0.11)	(0.13)	(0.15)	(0.27)	
Import taxes			-0.18**			
			(0.09)			
Export taxes			-0.14***			
			(0.08)			
Black market premium (/100)				-0.57**	-0.52**	
				(0.24)	(0.24)	
Nontariff barriers					0.02	
					(0.03)	
Log income (/100)	-1.32	-1.74**	-1.36***	-1.66***	-3.98**	-5.19**
	(0.81)	(0.82)	(0.79)	(0.91)	(1.72)	(2.60)
Log population (/100)	-0.01	-0.16	-0.19	0.22	-0.44	
	(0.37)	(0.37)	(0.39)	(0.45)	(0.88)	
Access (/100)	-0.14	-1.29	-1.16	-1.38	-3.64***	
	(1.11)	(1.20)	(1.22)	(1.23)	(2.02)	
Tropics (/100)	-1.81	-2.27	-1.34	2.51	-35.4**	
	(1.37)	(1.49)	(1.59)	(1.67)	(16.3)	
Country dummies	no	no	no	no	no	yes
N	92	83	83	75	47	84
R²	0.08	0.13	0.13	0.15	0.29	0.05
Root MSE	0.04	0.04	0.04	0.04	0.05	

Notes: Robust standard errors are reported in parenthesis. Period dummies are included in all specifications (coefficients not shown). Levels of statistical significance are as follows:
  *99% level
 **95% level
***90% level

effects is introduced (column 5). Again, the terms of trade apparently play no role (results not shown).

The main conclusion to be drawn from these regressions is that trade policies matter in Sub-Saharan Africa, in determining both the volume of trade and the growth thereof. As suggested by economic theory, import restrictions act as export restrictions. The variation in the trade/GDP ratios among Sub-Saharan African countries can be explained well by a small number of determinants, namely income per capita, country size, geography, and trade policy. The variation in the *growth* of trade is not as well explained, but there is strong evidence that trade taxes play a significant role here as well.

. . . .

THE DETERMINANTS OF ECONOMIC GROWTH WITHIN AFRICA

■ THE SOURCES OF LOW GROWTH LEVELS in African countries have been scrutinized in a number of studies. Easterly and Levine (1997) and Sachs and Warner (1997) are two recent analyses that have received wide attention. These two papers reach somewhat different conclusions: Easterly and Levine emphasize the role of ethnic fragmentation and poor-quality institutions; Sachs and Warner stress closed trade policies and geography as significant growth impediments.

Here I focus on growth regressions limited to a Sub-Saharan sample of countries. An important motivation for restricting the sample in this way is the widespread feeling in Africa that the region is structurally so different from the rest of the world that global comparisons based on cross-regional data are not particularly meaningful. Indeed, many African policymakers believe that the lessons from East Asia or Latin America do not apply to them because the circumstances differ so much. But African countries surely can learn from each other, and an empirical approach that focuses on performance within the continent has greater credibility for that reason.

My basic conclusion is that a small number of fundamentals determine the bulk of the cross-national variation in long-term growth performance within Africa. These fundamentals are human resources, macroeconomic/fiscal policy (especially the ability to manage resource booms), demography, and a conditional convergence factor. These variables "explain" about 80 percent of the growth variation in Africa over the 1965-1990 period (Rodrik 1997c). I find that trade policies do not play a significant role in growth, either in the medium run or the long run. However, excessive levels of export taxation are an important contributor to the

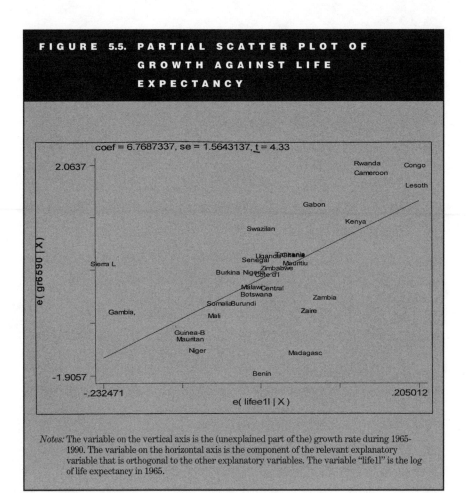

FIGURE 5.5. PARTIAL SCATTER PLOT OF GROWTH AGAINST LIFE EXPECTANCY

Notes: The variable on the vertical axis is the (unexplained part of the) growth rate during 1965-1990. The variable on the horizontal axis is the component of the relevant explanatory variable that is orthogonal to the other explanatory variables. The variable "life11" is the log of life expectancy in 1965.

relative decline of a few countries (namely, Uganda, Burundi, and Ghana). Partial scatter plots relating these variables to growth are shown in Figures 5.5 through 5.8. Movements in the external terms of trade are only weakly correlated with growth performance over the long run, but as discussed below, they play a more important role in the medium run (about a decade).

In Table 5.5, I present panel regressions where decade averages of per capita growth rates for the same three subperiods as before are regressed on their determinants. These regressions give a sense of the determinants of growth over the medium run (a decade), as opposed to the long run. The fit of these regressions is significantly worse than those for

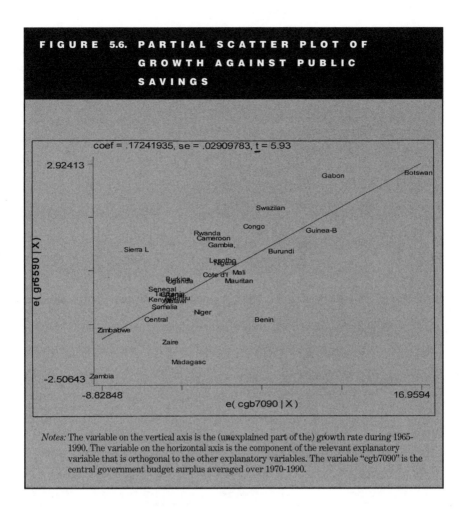

FIGURE 5.6. PARTIAL SCATTER PLOT OF GROWTH AGAINST PUBLIC SAVINGS

coef = .17241935, se = .02909783, t = 5.93

Notes: The variable on the vertical axis is the (unexplained part of the) growth rate during 1965-1990. The variable on the horizontal axis is the component of the relevant explanatory variable that is orthogonal to the other explanatory variables. The variable "cgb7090" is the central government budget surplus averaged over 1970-1990.

the long-run cross-sections, with an R^2 of 0.33 to 0.38. In particular, export taxation and demography are no longer statistically significant. Public savings and life expectancy (proxying for macroeconomic balance and human resources, respectively) remain significant. Changes in the terms of trade now enter with a highly significant coefficient, suggesting that this variable is an important determinant of growth over shorter horizons. The estimated coefficient suggests that a 10 percent improvement in the terms of trade per annum over a decade raises the annual average growth rate over the decade by 1.7 percentage points.

The final column of Table 5.5 provides some evidence that membership in the CFA zone has had asymmetric effects on growth in different

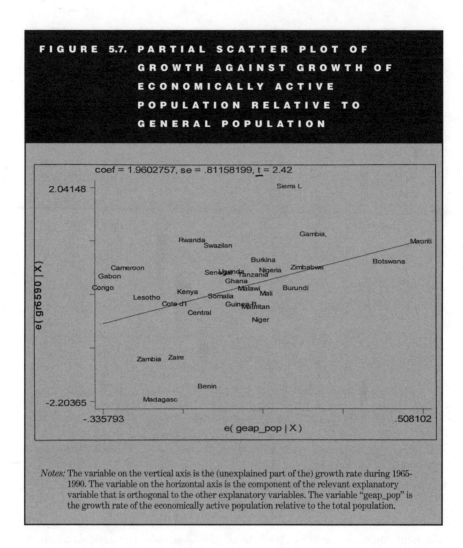

FIGURE 5.7. PARTIAL SCATTER PLOT OF GROWTH AGAINST GROWTH OF ECONOMICALLY ACTIVE POPULATION RELATIVE TO GENERAL POPULATION

coef = 1.9602757, se = .81158199, t = 2.42

Notes: The variable on the vertical axis is the (unexplained part of the) growth rate during 1965-1990. The variable on the horizontal axis is the component of the relevant explanatory variable that is orthogonal to the other explanatory variables. The variable "geap_pop" is the growth rate of the economically active population relative to the total population.

periods. When a dummy for CFA membership is interacted with the dummy for the 1975-1984 period (*cfa2*), the estimated coefficient is positive and borderline significant at the 95 percent level. But when the CFA dummy is interacted with the dummy for 1985-1994 (*cfa3*), the result is a negative coefficient that is significant at the 90 percent level. Hence, CFA membership increased growth in the earlier period (by an average of 2.3 percent per annum), but decreased it in the later period (by an average of 1.7 percent). The interpretation is that the fixed exchange-rate arrangement, and the price stability to which it gave rise, was an advantage when the underlying

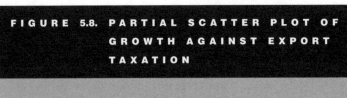

FIGURE 5.8. PARTIAL SCATTER PLOT OF GROWTH AGAINST EXPORT TAXATION

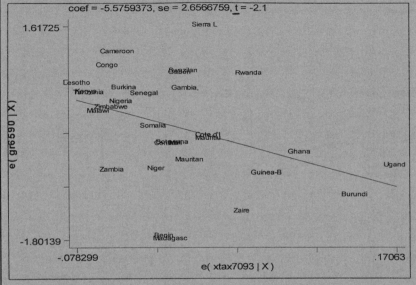

Notes: The variable on the vertical axis is the (unexplained part of the) growth rate during 1965-1990. The variable on the horizontal axis is the component of the relevant explanatory variable that is orthogonal to the other explanatory variables. The variable "xtax7093" is the average rate of export duties during 1970-1993.

external balances were sustainable, but became a hindrance when devaluations were called for later.

. . . .

COUNTRY EXPERIENCES[15]

THE BENEFITS OF OPENNESS: BOTSWANA

Botswana's economy has benefited greatly from openness. Its phenomenal economic performance has been based on diamond exports. But

TABLE 5.5. GROWTH REGRESSIONS

| | Dependent variable: per capita GDP growth | | | |
	(1)	(2)	(3)	(4)
Export taxes	-1.65 (3.07)			
Log initial GDP per capita	-1.13*** (0.65)	-1.44* (0.45)	-1.61* (0.48)	-1.42* (0.46)
Life expectancy	0.16* (0.05)	0.19* (0.04)	0.14* (0.04)	0.19* (0.04)
Public savings (x100)	0.12** (0.06)			
Growth of economically active population (relative to total)	0.30 (0.85)			
Terms-of-trade growth		0.17* (0.06)	0.17* (0.07)	0.18* (0.06)
Botswana			3.35** (1.64)	
Mauritius			2.31 (1.80)	
cfa2				2.33*** (1.21)
cfa3				-1.72*** (1.01)
N	78	115	115	115
R²	0.33	0.34	0.38	0.38
Root MSE	0.03	0.02	0.02	0.02

Notes: Period dummies included (coefficents not shown). Robust standard errors are reported in parenthesis. Levels of statistical significance are as follows:
  *99% level
 **95% level
***90% level

because natural resources in and of themselves are not always a blessing, as too many African countries have discovered, there is much more to this success story than diamonds. As the growth regressions discussed above suggest, the proximate determinants of Botswana's distinctive performance are prudent fiscal and macroeconomic policies, relatively well-developed human resources, and an early demographic transition that reduced the dependency ratio. These factors enabled a sharp increase in investment rates in the early 1970s, mainly in mining. But also noteworthy is that the government has managed the diamond boom remarkably well: resources have not been wasted, and temporary reversals in export receipts (as in 1981 and 1982) have been met with quick adjustments in the exchange rate and fiscal policy.

Superior governance in macroeconomic management has apparently been matched in other fields as well. As mentioned before, Botswana is one of Africa's few continuous democracies. The bureaucracy is honest and competent, attaches great value to economic expertise, and has consistently produced sensible macroeconomic policies. There has been no large-scale urban bias and no white elephants (Harvey 1992, p. 348). However, the government's philosophy has been far from laissez-faire. Government expenditures stood above 50 percent of GDP by the early 1990s, one of the highest levels in the world. Spending on public investment, subsidies, and other economic functions made up 40 to 50 percent of these expenditures. As a result, as Harvey notes, "there were enormous improvements in the provision of health and education, in the building of infrastructure and in other government services" (p. 339).

What has distinguished economic interventions in Botswana is the quality, not the quantity, of the interventions. Why this has been so is not altogether clear. As in Mauritius, the initial conditions were not favorable. When it became independent in 1966, Botswana was one of the poorest countries in the world, lacking a capital city and an educational base, and having only a few miles of paved roads (Harvey 1992, p. 338). Furthermore, Botswana has been virtually surrounded by warfare and violence, as a consequence of wars of independence and civil conflicts in Angola, Zimbabwe, and Namibia, and the antiapartheid struggle in South Africa.

One common explanation for Botswana's success is the rural origin of the political leadership. Harvey (1992), for example, emphasizes the

strong influence of rural exporters on economic policy. A large majority of politicians and senior government officials in Botswana own cattle, and an even higher proportion are related to people who own cattle. The income from cattle comes mostly from exporting. (pp. 360-361)

This, it is argued, explains why policies in Botswana have not been antiexport, and why the economy has never been allowed to succumb to the Dutch disease.

An alternative hypothesis focuses on the external constraints on trade policy. Along with Lesotho, Swaziland, and South Africa, Botswana has long been a member of the Southern Africa Customs Union (SACU). This means that Botswana has no independent trade policy; goods circulate freely between it and South Africa. The government gets a share of customs revenue collected by South Africa, which amounts to around 20 percent of the value of Botswana's imports, a high level. What matters from our perspective is that government officials have no control over this revenue on a day-to-day basis; nor do they have an ability to interfere with the flow of goods from South Africa. More to the point, domestic producers in the urban areas *know* that this is so and therefore realize that lobbying policy-makers for favors in the trade arena is futile. We can think of the absence of an independent trade policy as an extreme form of an "agency of restraint" (Collier 1995).[16]

Could this externally imposed free-trade regime be a key reason for Botswana's success on the economic front? Obviously, the government's ability to tax exports, either directly or indirectly, was sharply restricted. But beyond that, the absence of an import-substituting urban lobby— ensured by the free-trade regime—could have led to improved governance on other fronts as well. For example, the admirable manner in which the government responded to a large drop in diamond earnings in 1981, by swiftly devaluing the currency and avoiding exchange controls (see Lewis 1993, pp. 19ff), may have been enabled by the absence of entrenched urban interests. Protected behind nontariff barriers, these urban groups would have welcomed such controls and other trade restrictions and would have made it more difficult for the government to undertake the requisite policy adjustments. In any case, that was the typical experience in the rest of Africa and Latin America, where the governments responded to external shocks by tightening restrictions and delaying macroeconomic adjustments.

Therefore, one interpretation of Botswana's experience is that governance was improved not only by democracy but by the absence of an administered trade regime. In this case, imported institutions seem to have helped.

Ghana and Uganda undertook a broad range of reforms during the 1980s, including extensive trade liberalization, after a prolonged period of economic decline.[17] In both countries, all major economic indicators had sunk to distressingly low levels by the early 1980s, and for both the culprit was gross mismanagement of the economy, aggravated by civil war in the case of Uganda during 1985-86.

Extensive trade reforms began in Ghana in 1983, and in Uganda in 1987. Previously the trade regime in each country had been characterized by a plethora of trade control instruments: high tariffs, stringent quota restrictions (QRs), export restrictions, foreign-exchange restrictions, and a high black-market premium. In both countries, the reforms initially focused on removing the extreme distortions in the market for foreign exchange. In Ghana, there were three devaluations over a three-year period and a steady, if slow, reduction in the gap between the official and parallel market rates. An auction market for foreign exchange was introduced in 1986, and the unification of the exchange rate was finally accomplished the following year. In Uganda, following an initial 77 percent devaluation in 1987, the shilling was adjusted periodically throughout 1989, and the parallel-market premium steadily declined. Foreign-exchange bureaus were licensed in 1990, further narrowing the spread between the parallel and official markets. Finally, at the end of 1993, the exchange system was unified with the introduction of an interbank system.

With regard to QRs, the introduction of a new licensing system in Ghana in 1986 allowed the importation of nonconsumer goods without restriction. Import licensing was streamlined by movement from a positive list to a short negative list. In 1989, import licensing and prohibitions were fully terminated. In Uganda, import liberalization was fairly rapid, beginning with the open general licensing scheme (OGL) in 1987, which focused on allocating foreign exchange for the importation of raw materials on a "nondiscriminatory" basis. The list of eligible firms was expanded periodically throughout 1990. By 1993, the OGL scheme had been phased out and replaced with a short negative list.

In both countries there were several rounds of tariff reforms, some aimed at rationalizing the tariff structure and others (especially in Ghana) aimed at making up for some of the protection lost through the reform of the QRs. Overall, the ranges of tariffs and their dispersion have been greatly reduced.

On the export side Uganda went farther, removing the monopoly of the coffee-marketing board and abolishing all export taxes (including the tax on coffee, which was reintroduced in 1994 following a rise in world prices). Ghana has reduced taxes on cocoa exports, but the government retains its export monopoly.

There can be little doubt that these reforms, along with better macroeconomic management and external financial support, have helped Ghana and Uganda recover. Both countries' economies are growing after a long period of decline. Exports are up in both countries, and in the case of Ghana the export/GDP ratio exceeds the level reached in 1970, even though per capita GDP still falls short of the 1970 level. Investment is up as well but is apparently led primarily by public investment. At the same time, it is evident that even after a decade or more of reform, there remains some doubt about the long-run performance of the two economies. Neither has yet caught up with the level of per capita income reached in 1970. It is too early to declare victory.

REFORM WITHOUT GROWTH: MALI AND GAMBIA

Mali and Gambia provide an interesting contrast with the experience of Ghana and Uganda. The economies of both Mali and Gambia are now substantially open to external trade.[18] However, they have yet to reap significant growth gains, partly because of extremely poor human and physical resources, and their growth potential remains low. Another factor is that their reforms did not come after a protracted period of decline, at least of the order of magnitude experienced by Ghana and Uganda, and therefore they have not had the benefit of a rebound in economic activity.

Mali began its trade reforms in 1986 by eliminating export monopolies. In 1988, the reforms were significantly strengthened with quota liberalization and abolition of import monopolies. In 1990, all QRs and import-licensing requirements were abolished, and the following year import tariffs were reduced to a range of 6 to 41 percent. Until the devaluation of the CFA franc in January 1994, however, the economy was stuck with an uncompetitive exchange rate. There have been signs of economic revival since the devaluation.

Gambia has traditionally been an open economy, free of import quotas and other trade restrictions on any good other than groundnuts (Hadjimichael et al. 1992). Facing a payments crisis, the government launched a macroeconomic stabilization and adjustment program in mid-1985. The key components of the program were the liberalization of the exchange rate, increases in the prices of traded goods, particularly groundnuts, and the elimination of government subsidies. Tariffs were rationalized, and the average duty rate was reduced. In 1990, the state export monopoly for groundnuts was eliminated, and farmers and traders were allowed to sell groundnuts to anyone willing to buy.

Hence, there has been substantial trade reform in both Mali and Gambia, perhaps more than in Ghana and Uganda. But there is little indication that either economy has been greatly boosted by these measures. In both Mail and Gambia, export ratios have generally increased following the reforms, but the impact on economic growth has been modest at best. These cases support the finding from the cross-national regressions: trade policy has strong and predictable effects on trade volumes, but it is an unreliable instrument for generating economic growth.

· ·

CONCLUSION

■ THE TURBULENCE IN WORLD MARKETS that began in the mid-1970s had severe adverse effects on both Latin America and Africa. The upshot in Latin America was the wholesale adoption by virtually all governments in the region of orthodox recipes—namely fiscal retrenchment, deregulation, free trade, and privatization. In Sub-Saharan Africa, free-market religion has found far fewer converts. Despite tremendous pressure from donor governments and multilateral agencies, African policymakers have generally been more skeptical about the value of opening up their economies and reducing the role of government. Consequently, reforms have progressed gradually and have been full of interruptions and reversals. The contrast with Latin America, where governments have stuck with ambitious reforms even under severe macroeconomic difficulties—for example during the Mexican peso crisis of 1995—is striking.

Some consensus exists on what constitutes a reasonable trade strategy for African countries. The consensus can be crudely expressed in terms of several do's and one don't's: *do* demonopolize trade; *do* streamline the import regime, reduce red tape, and implement transparent customs procedures; *do* replace quantitative restrictions with tariffs; *do* avoid extreme variations in tariff rates and excessively high rates of effective protection; *do* allow exporters duty-free access to imported inputs; *do* refrain from large doses of antiexport bias; *don't* tax export crops too highly. Provided that the qualifiers in this list of guidelines ("extreme," "excessively high," etc.) are interpreted reasonably, these desiderata remain useful. They also leave considerable room for policymakers to make their own choices over a wide range of trade and industrial policy options. To take one example: an African country with average tariffs of 35 percent will have made a very different choice than one with average tariffs of five percent, yet both countries would be regarded as having an "open" trade regime according to Sachs and Warner's (1995) influential measure of openness.[19]

Some aggressive reformers, such as Ghana and Uganda (and Mauritius before them), have implemented most, but not all, of the above agenda. Many other countries have done much less. Part of the reticence among African policymakers results from the suspicion that trade reform may not "work" in Sub-Saharan Africa, at least the way it "worked" in East Asia and more recently in some cases in Latin America.

I have argued in this chapter that there is little ground for pessimism in regard to trade reform. The evidence indicates that the cross-national variation in trade performance *within* the region is well explained by the standard determinants of trade, namely trade policies, income levels, country size, and geography. In particular, trade policies, as measured by taxation of imports and exports, are significantly and robustly correlated with volumes of trade as well as the growth of trade. Removal of these impediment to trade can be expected to have a major impact on trade volumes.

However, a second theme is that commercial policy reforms have only weak links to economic growth. The variation in long-term growth performance within the region is explained largely by investment rates, human resources, fiscal policy, demography, and a catch-up factor. The external terms of trade have also played a role over shorter horizons. Trade policies have played a much smaller role in growth performance, although there is evidence that excessive taxation of exports was partly responsible for some dismal failures.

I have shown that the marginalization of Africa in world trade is mostly due to the slow growth of African economies. Taken as a whole, the region participates in international trade as much as can be expected according to international benchmarks relating trade volumes to income levels, country size, and geography.

The two most successful countries in the region, Botswana and Mauritius, have combined elements of an open economy with less orthodox policies in other spheres. As a member of SACU, Botswana has not had an independent trade policy, a factor that may have been crucial in achieving good governance on macroeconomic front and elsewhere. But Botswana has also had a very large public sector and extensive government involvement in the economy. As I discussed in Chapter 3, Mauritius followed a two-track strategy until the 1980s, with an export processing zone operating on free-trade principles functioning side by side with a highly protected domestic economy. Mauritius and Botswana illustrate the argument that, as Helleiner (1997) has said, "African governments need not succumb to 'mindless globalization' via their total abandonment of any role in the mediation of national links to the world economy" (p. 37).

Successful cases such as Botswana and Mauritius notwithstanding, trade reform in Africa has generally been erratic and marked by reversals and lack of credibility. At the heart of these difficulties lie the sharp distributional consequences of trade reform. The fault lines exist not only between the rural sector (the likely beneficiary of the removal of export restrictions) and the urban sector, but between the public sector (where bureaucratic privileges and rents reside) and the private sector. Managing these distributional issues is tricky, yet it is crucial to successful reform (Rodrik forthcoming 1998c).

Clearly, Sub-Saharan African countries are able to grow at rapid rates when the circumstances are right. Trade volumes are responsive to prices, and countries where exports of traditional and nontraditional products have been sharply discouraged by taxes and other restrictions can expect a solid payoff in terms of trade volumes when such policies are removed. There is no evidence that African trade has been significantly affected by external developments. And there is little ground for concern in general that the structure of African economies makes them unsuitable for the application of remedies that have worked in other settings.

At the same time, there are clear limits to what trade policy, or outward orientation, can accomplish. Growth depends foremost on the fundamentals identified above. Reaping the benefits of investments in human resources and infrastructure and establishing the credibility of the institutions of macroeconomic management are both going to take time. So will the demographic transition. Opening an economy to international trade is not a quick fix that can substitute for these harder tasks. As I suggested in the introduction to this chapter, a heavy emphasis on trade liberalization can backfire if it diverts the scarce energies and political resources of government leaders from growth fundamentals. The benefits of trade reform should not be oversold. Economic policy should focus on growth, not on trade.

NOTES

[1] Parts of this chapter draw heavily on Rodrik (1997c).

[2] According to World Bank data, these are the Central African Republic, Chad, Ghana, Madagascar, Niger, Rwanda, Senegal, Sudan, Tanzania, and Zambia.

[3] This is based on internationally comparable statistics from the Penn World Tables.

[4] As in the previous chapter, growth during 1960-1975 and log per capita GDP in 1975 have been included as additional right-hand-side variables. The variable on the vertical axis, as before, is the difference in growth rates between the two periods (1975-1989 minus 1960-1975).

[5] See Brautigam (1997) for a useful account.

[6] See also the recent paper by Collier (1998), which emphasizes the positive role of democracy in managing conflict in ethnically divided African societies.

[7] In Rodrik (1997c), I report similar results where the dependent variable is the sum of exports and imports in GDP at internationally comparable prices.

[8] One might ask how this result is consistent with the evidence that 1) trade barriers remain, on average, higher in Africa (as discussed before), and 2) trade barriers do have significant negative effects on trade volumes in Africa (as will be shown shortly). The answer must lie in other characteristics specific to Africa, which on their own would have boosted trade volumes beyond what is "normal" by cross-country benchmarks. The continent's excessive reliance on natural resource exports is one plausible candidate. Note, moreover, that this finding does not preclude the possibility that many African countries significantly undertrade.

[9] "If anything, the average African country tends to overtrade compared with developing countries in other regions, although the degree to which Africa overtrades has steadily declined over the past two and one-half decades" (Coe and Hoffmaister 1998, p. 6). Wood and Mayer (1998) have analyzed a different but related question: Is the structure of exports in Africa, especially the low share of manufactures, an outlier relative to cross-country norms? Their finding is that the low share of manufactures is mostly related to Africa's unusual combination of a low level of human resources with high levels of natural resources.

[10] The conventional wisdom holds commercial policies responsible. Yeats, for example, lays the blame for Africa's marginalization in trade on domestic interventions in the areas of trade policy and transport policy. He concludes: "If Africa is to reverse its unfavorable export trends, it must quickly adopt trade and structural adjustment policies that enhance its international competitiveness and allow African exporters to capitalize on opportunities in foreign markets" (1997, p. 24). Similarly, Collier links the declining importance of Africa in world trade to the fact that "its economies have become more inward-looking while all other economies have become more integrated into the world economy" (1995, p. 541).

[11] For more details, see Rodrik (1997c).

[12] The only countries for which the measure *tropics* is less than 1.0 are Botswana (0.5), Lesotho (0.0), Madagascar (0.9), Mauritania (0.8), and Swaziland (0.0). One could also read this variable as a dummy for SACU (South African Customs Union). However, adding a separate dummy for SACU countries (Botswana, Lesotho, and Swaziland) does not affect the magnitude and statistical significance of the coefficient on *tropics*.

[13] In addition, there is an econometric problem. The dependent variable, which is the volume of trade (as a share of GDP), enters the construction of the trade-tax measure in the denominator. This raises the possibility of a spurious negative correlation between the two variables. But there are reasons to believe that this is not a serious source of bias. For example, I find that import taxes tend to depress export volumes (as well as the growth of exports), even though the construction of these two variables is independent. Also, the results are quite similar using partner-country trade data (reported in Rodrik 1997c).

[14] In practice, there are some good reasons why the Lerner theorem need not apply perfectly, including complications that arise from unbalanced trade and the difficulty of calculating equivalences in a multigood world with varying tariff/subsidy rates. See Helleiner (1995) for a useful practical discussion of the issues.

[15] This section is based on Rodrik (1997c and 1998c).

[16] As a small country in SACU, Botswana was essentially forced to inherit South Africa's relative price structure. Its gains from trade derived from the difference between this relative-price structure and that which would have obtained under autarky in Botswana. The fact that the external tariffs in SACU were fairly high—and that South Africa's relative structure was distorted relative to the rest of the world—is largely irrelevant to the existence of gains from trade for Botswana. However, to the extent that the external tariffs in SACU pushed South Africa's relative prices in the direction of Botswana's autarky price ratio, these external tariffs reduced Botswana's gains from trade (relative to free trade outside the SACU structure).

[17] This account relies on Dean, Desai, and Riedel, (1994), Tutu and Oduro (1996), Hadjimichael, Nowak, Sharer, and Tahari (1996), Ssemogerere (1997), World Bank (1996a, 1996b), and WTO (1995).

[18] This account is based on World Bank (1996a), Dean et al. (1994), Hadjimichael, Rumbaugh, and Verreydt (1992), Radelet (1993), and Sahn (1994).

[19] Sachs and Warner (1995) set their cutoff level for "openness" at 40 percent where average tariffs are concerned. Their measure of openness relies on four other indicators besides tariffs.

Chapter 6
Summary and
Implications

A MODERN-DAY FABLE

■   IMAGINE THAT A MARTIAN LANDS IN WASHINGTON and is captured
by a group of mischievous economists. The economists make a deal with her.
They will release her if she can prove her intelligence by correctly answering
an economics question: Which government policies are most likely to pre-
dict how well different countries did over the last two decades? To make the
deal fair, the economists agree to provide the Martian with a briefing book
containing a set of readings drawn from the current literature on trade and
development. After this crash course on contemporary economic thought, the
Martian provides her answer. The countries that grew most rapidly, she
replies, were the ones with low tariffs, few nontariff barriers, and no restrictions on international capital flows. The economists look at each other and
realize that they have no choice but to release her. They conclude that intelligent life exists outside Planet Earth.

Bit by the economics bug, the Martian decides to learn a bit more
before returning home. She reads up on statistics and gets hold of some
cross-national data. She calculates the correlation coefficients between
various indicators of trade policy and growth of GDP per capita across
countries. But the results are puzzling. None of the indicators of policy
toward trade and capital flows that she can lay her hands on—average tariff
levels, nontariff coverage ratios, or indexes of capital-account liberalization—
correlate statistically significantly with per capita GDP growth.[1] Either
economics is a lot more complicated than she sensed, or else humans are not
nearly as intelligent as they seem. In either case, she figures it is best to leave
Earth before her captors change their minds.

. . . .

THE PROMISE AND PERILS OF OPENNESS

■   FOR POLICYMAKERS AROUND THE WORLD, the appeal of opening up
to global markets is based on a simple but powerful promise: international
economic integration will improve economic performance. As countries
reduce their tariff and nontariff barriers to trade and open up to international

capital flows, the expectation is that economic growth will increase. This, in turn, will reduce poverty and improve the quality of life for the vast majority of the residents of developing nations.

The trouble, as the Martian discovered, is that there is no convincing evidence that openness, in the sense of low barriers to trade and capital flows, systematically produces these consequences. In practice, the links between openness and economic growth tend to be weak, and to be contingent on the presence of complementary policies and institutions. As I emphasized in Chapter 2, the benefits of openness lie on the import side: the ability to import ideas, investment goods, and intermediate inputs from more advanced countries can significantly boost economic growth. But to realize this potential, developing nations need other things too. They need to create an environment that is conducive to private investment—to follow what I have called an investment strategy. They need to improve their institutions of conflict management—legally guaranteed civil liberties and political freedoms, social partnerships, and social insurance—so that they can maintain macroeconomic stability and adjust to rapid changes in external circumstances. In the absence of these complements to a strategy of external liberalization, openness will not yield much. At worst, it will cause instability, widening inequalities, and social conflict.

The evidence from the experience of the last two decades is clear: the countries whose economies have grown most rapidly since the mid-1970s are those that have invested a large share of GDP and maintained macroeconomic stability. This is the bottom line of the cross-national econometric exercise summarized in Table 6.1. The exercise is the type of effort that the Martian might have undertaken, had she a bit more knowledge and time. Her findings with regard to the relative insignificance of trade policy, however, would remain unchanged.

Table 6.1 shows the consequences of regressing per capita GDP growth over the 1975-1994 period on initial income, initial education levels, regional dummies, and additional explanatory variables. As the table shows, there is only a weak correlation over this period between economic growth and indicators of openness. Whether based on tariff and nontariff restrictions or on trade volumes, none of the measures of trade openness exhibit a statistically significant relationship with growth (columns 5, 6, and 7).[2]

Openness to capital flows—captured by an indicator of capital-account liberalization—does not exert any influence either (column 8). Neither is the size of government a significant factor (columns 9 and 10).

TABLE 6.1. DETERMINANTS OF PER CAPITA GDP GROWTH, 1975-1994

	(1)	(2)	(3)	(4)	(5)	(6)	(7)	(8)	(9)	(10)
Latin America	-0.016* (0.004)	-0.014* (0.004)	-0.014* (0.004)	-0.011* (0.003)	-0.018* (0.004)	-0.018* (0.004)	-0.018* (0.004)	-0.016* (0.004)	-0.017* (0.004)	-0.015** (0.006)
East Asia	0.024* (0.008)	0.021* (0.007)	0.020** (0.008)	0.021* (0.008)	0.016*** (0.009)	0.024* (0.008)	0.022* (0.008)	0.021** (0.009)	0.022* (0.007)	0.017*** (0.009)
Sub-Saharan Africa	-0.017* (0.006)	-0.017* (0.006)	-0.016** (0.006)	-0.018* (0.005)	-0.021* (0.006)	-0.024* (0.005)	-0.024* (0.005)	-0.017* (0.006)	-0.017* (0.006)	-0.021* (0.007)
Log per capita GDP, 1975	-0.003 (0.003)	-0.004*** (0.003)	-0.005*** (0.003)	-0.006*** (0.003)	-0.005 (0.004)	-0.006*** (0.003)	-0.006*** (0.003)	-0.003 (0.003)	-0.004 (0.003)	-0.004 (0.003)
Log secondary enrollment, 1975	0.005*** (0.003)	0.006** (0.003)	0.007** (0.003)	0.006** (0.002)	0.005*** (0.003)	0.008* (0.003)	0.007** (0.003)	0.005*** (0.003)	0.005*** (0.003)	0.004 (0.002)
Investment										
Investment/GDP, 1975-1994		0.095* (0.025)								
Excluding Lesotho[a]			0.110** (0.050)							
Macroeconomic stability										
Index of macromismanagement[b]				-0.026* (0.007)						
Openness										
Average tariff rate[c] (x100)					-0.024 (0.031)					

Continued on next page

TABLE 6.1. DETERMINANTS OF PER CAPITA GDP GROWTH, 1975-1994

	(1)	(2)	(3)	(4)	(5)	(6)	(7)	(8)	(9)	(10)
(Continued)										
Nontariff barrier (NTB) coverage ratio[c]						-0.009 (0.009)				
Trade[d]							0.000 (0.000)			
Capital-account liberalization[e]								0.002 (0.005)		
Government size										
Government consumption/GDP									-0.040 (0.025)	
Total government expenditures/GDP										-0.011 (0.021)
N	91	84	83	83	82	73	73	90	91	76
R²	0.45	0.56	0.56	0.53	0.42	0.61	0.59	0.43	0.47	0.40

Notes:

a. This regression is run with and without Lesotho, as this country looks like an outlier that could distort the results.

b. This index is constructed by taking a simple average of the inflation rate and the log of (1 plus) the black market premium during 1975-1990.

c. Sources: World Development Indicators 1998 (average import: duty rate, 1975-1994) and Barro and Lee (1994) for NTBs.

d. The volume of trade in excess of the predicted volume, with the predicted values coming from a cross-country regression of trade on geographical determinants (population, distance from major trading partners, and regional dummies).

e. The proportion of years during 1975-1994 without restrictions on the capital account, as coded by Kim (1997) from IMF sources.

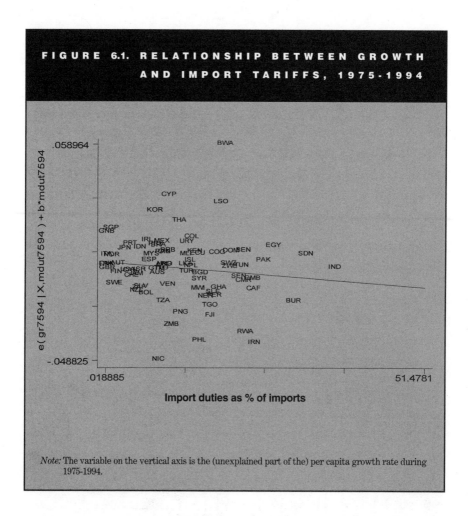

FIGURE 6.1. RELATIONSHIP BETWEEN GROWTH AND IMPORT TARIFFS, 1975-1994

Note: The variable on the vertical axis is the (unexplained part of the) per capita growth rate during 1975-1994.

What matters most are investment rates (columns 2 and 3) and macro-economic stability (column 4).

The scatter plots in Figures 6.1 through 6.5 give a visual sense of these results. They show the relationship between economic growth and some of these policy variables, after the effects of other influences (initial income, education, and regional dummies) are taken out. The weakness of the association between indicators of openness and economic growth is evident in the scatter plots that constitute Figures 6.1 through 6.3. For instance, Pakistan and Egypt have done comparably well in their regions despite high average tariffs, Haiti has done very poorly despite low nontariff barriers, and Bolivia has done dismally despite having an open capital account through-

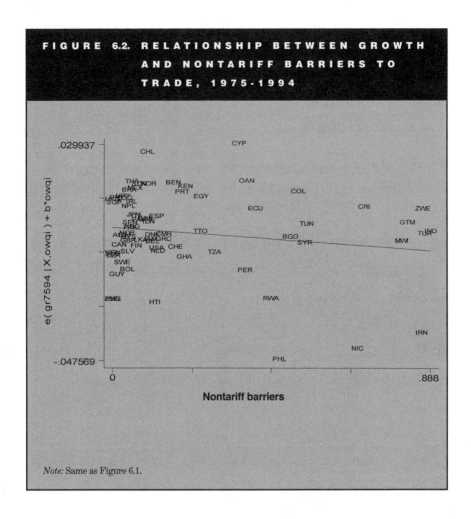

FIGURE 6.2. RELATIONSHIP BETWEEN GROWTH AND NONTARIFF BARRIERS TO TRADE, 1975-1994

Note: Same as Figure 6.1.

out most of the 1975-1994 period. The relationship between growth and investment is much tighter, as is the relationship between growth and macroeconomic stability (see Figures 6.4 and 6.5).[3]

Such findings should caution policymakers against buying too readily into current development fashions. The evidence in favor of the small government/free trade orthodoxy is less than overwhelming. Investment and macroeconomic policies remain key. There is no magic formula for surmounting the challenges of economic growth—and if there is, openness is not it.

From a broader historical perspective, there should be nothing surprising about these conclusions, and in particular about the argument that

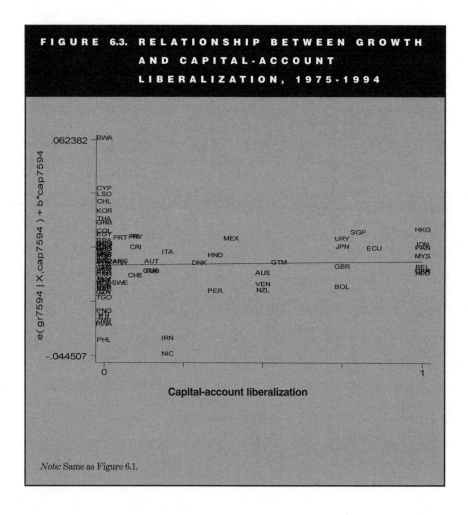

FIGURE 6.3. RELATIONSHIP BETWEEN GROWTH AND CAPITAL-ACCOUNT LIBERALIZATION, 1975-1994

Note: Same as Figure 6.1.

the relationship between trade barriers and economic performance is ambiguous. After all, most of the countries that successfully followed Britain into the Industrial Revolution did so under trade regimes that would be classified as highly restrictive by today's standards. In the United States, to take a prominent example, import tariffs averaged around 40 percent in the half century following the Civil War, a period in which the United States caught up with and overtook Britain and the rest of Europe. To put this number in perspective, note that only one country in our sample (among those for which there is data) had an average tariff rate during 1975-1994 exceeding 40 percent (Seychelles)—although nontariff barriers are more common these days than they were during the 19th century.[4] Neither history nor recent

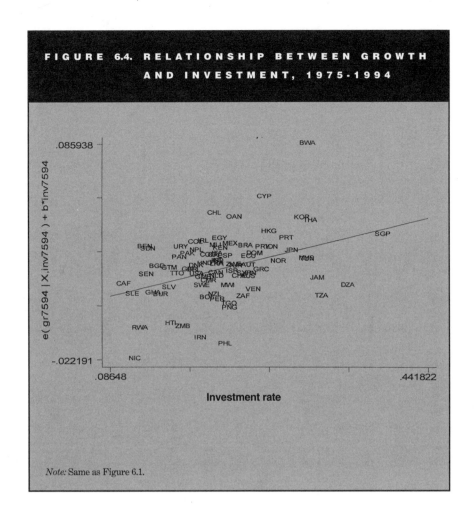

FIGURE 6.4. RELATIONSHIP BETWEEN GROWTH AND INVESTMENT, 1975-1994

Investment rate

Note: Same as Figure 6.1.

evidence provides support for a straightforward association between the level of trade barriers and long-term growth.

. . . .

HOW MUCH IS REALLY KNOWN ABOUT ECONOMIC POLICIES FOR SUSTAINABLE GROWTH?

■   IN LATE 1997, SOUTH KOREA BECAME THE LATEST VICTIM of the Asian financial crisis. With foreign reserves in danger of depletion, the South

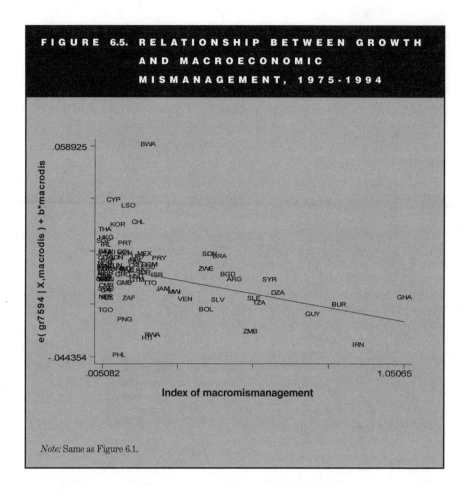

FIGURE 6.5. RELATIONSHIP BETWEEN GROWTH AND MACROECONOMIC MISMANAGEMENT, 1975-1994

Note: Same as Figure 6.1.

Korean government approached the IMF for help. To help stave off the crisis, the IMF organized a rescue package of $57 billion from official sources, including $21 billion of its own money. In return, the South Korean government accepted an extensive program of reform that, carried to its fruition, would completely overhaul the structure and governance of the South Korean economy. The program included:

- a comprehensive financial-sector restructuring, including the provision of independence to the central bank and the suspension of operations of nine merchant banks;

- tight-money policies, higher interest rates, and a fiscal retrenchment initially equivalent to about 2 percent of GDP (the latter requirement was subsequently relaxed as the real economy deteriorated more than anticipated);

- the dismantling of "nontransparent and inefficient ties among the government, banks, and businesses," including the phasing out of the system of cross-guarantees within conglomerates;

- a program of trade liberalization, including the phasing out of trade-related subsidies, of restrictive import licensing, and of the import diversification program;

- capital-account liberalization, including the lifting of all capital-account restrictions on foreign investors' access to the South Korean bond market; and

- labor market reforms increasing flexibility (i.e., rules to make layoffs easier).[5]

How appropriate were these measures? As Feldstein (1998, p.25) has argued, what South Korea needed most at the time "was coordinated action by creditor banks to restructure its short-term debts, lengthening their maturity and providing additional temporary credits to help meet the interest obligations." There is little reason to believe, as Feldstein emphasizes, that most of the structural changes imposed by the IMF on South Korea were required for renewed access to capital markets:

> Although many of the structural reforms that the IMF included in its early-December program for Korea would probably improve the long-term performance of the Korean economy, they are not needed for Korea to gain access to capital markets. They are also among the most politically sensitive issues: labor market rules, regulations of corporate structure and governance, government-business relations, and international trade. The specific policies that the IMF insists must be changed are not so different from those in the major countries of Europe: labor market rules that cause 12 percent unemployment, corporate ownership structures that give banks and governments controlling interests in industrial companies, state subsidies to inefficient and loss-making industries, and trade barriers that restrict Japanese auto imports to a trickle and block foreign purchases of industrial companies. (Feldstein 1998, pp.27-28)

In effect, the financial crisis was treated as an opportunity to remold the South Korean economy in the image of a free-market economy—or more correctly, a Washington economist's idea of one. That the IMF could get away with this—remember that the South Korean government enthusiastically latched on to most elements of the program—is indicative of a number of novel developments in the world economy. First, even the most successful countries in the world can be brought to their knees nowadays by sudden changes in market sentiment. Second, international institutions such as the IMF (and the U.S. government as their principal backer) can acquire tremendous leverage over the policies of smaller countries when the world economy turns sour. Third, global policymakers have come to place excessive confidence in a particular vision of what constitutes desirable economic policy. This neoliberal model of the economy emphasizes free trade and free markets, with the government's role limited to the provision of the rule of law, prudential regulation, and minimal social safety nets.

"Imposing detailed economic prescriptions on legitimate governments would remain questionable," Feldstein (1998, pp.28-29) writes,

> even if economists were unanimous about the best way to reform the countries' economic policies. In practice, however, there are substantial disagreements about what should be done. Even when there has been near unanimity about the appropriate economic policies, the consensus has changed radically. After all, the IMF was created to defend and manage a fixed exchange-rate system that is now regarded as economically inappropriate and practically unworkable. Similarly, for a long time the advice to developing countries that came from the World Bank, the IMF's sister institution, and from leading academic specialists emphasized national plans for government-managed industrial development. The official and very influential U.N. Economic Commission for Latin America preached the virtues of protectionist policies to block industrial imports in order to encourage countries to develop their own manufacturing industries. Now the consensus of professional economists and international agencies calls for the opposite policies: flexible exchange rates, market-determined economic development, and free trade.... Even if it were desirable for Korea to shift toward labor, goods, and capital markets more like those of the United States, it may be best to evolve in that direction more gradually and with fewer shocks to existing businesses.

As Feldstein recognizes, the fact that fashions in economic policy change frequently should make us more humble in prescribing detailed structural programs to developing countries—especially those that have grown rich by eschewing conventional wisdom and espousing heterodox policies. The reality is that our prescriptions often go far beyond what can be supported by careful theoretical reasoning or empirical demonstration. We know a lot less about what makes for good economic policy than we recognize.

As I have discussed throughout this book, the economies that have done well in the postwar period have all succeeded through their own particular brand of heterodox policies. Macroeconomic stability and high investment rates have been common, but beyond that, many details differ. This too should be a warning against trying to fit all developing nations into a straitjacket of policies that have only recently become conventional wisdom.

. . . .

INTERNATIONAL CONSTRAINTS
ON NATIONAL POLICY

■   BUT DO DEVELOPING COUNTRIES REALLY HAVE A CHOICE? Can small nations still pursue their own distinctive agendas and govern their economies in ways that differ from the prevailing precepts? To hear many policymakers speak, the answer is no. It has become a common refrain that there is little choice but to privatize, open up, and attract DFI.

As I have argued before, exports and DFI are means to an end, not ends in themselves. Gearing economic policy toward performance in the external sectors of the economy, at the expense of other objectives, amounts to mixing up the ends and the means of economic policy. Furthermore, there is nothing more conducive to trade and DFI than strong economic growth itself. Foreign investors care little about Botswana's huge public sector, and neither are they much deterred by Chinese-style socialism. Policies that are successful in igniting growth are also likely to pay off in terms of "international competitiveness."

As I have argued above, external constraints can sometimes be useful in fostering economic development if policymakers use these constraints wisely and creatively. For a government that would otherwise make a mess of its tariff code, the ability to bind tariffs in the World Trade Organization represents a useful opportunity. In an economy with a tendency toward large fiscal deficits, the discipline imposed by international financial markets can enhance the prospects for macroeconomic stability. The harmonization of regulatory standards with those in the advanced industrial countries can impart the rule of law and increase transparency in developing countries.

Yet such externally induced disciplines can also backfire if they are inappropriate to the economy in question or are viewed as serving the needs of particular social groups at the expense of others. Two conditions must be met to ensure that this does not happen:

1. The decision to submit to external discipline—by signing on to international agreements, opening up markets to international competition, or accepting World Bank/IMF conditionality—must be the product of a democratic decision-making process, with broad participation from major social groups.

2. There must be solid evidence that the discipline in question will improve economic performance in the country submitting to it.

International policy regimes that significantly constrain the ability of national policymakers to choose their own paths are likely to prove counterproductive in the absence of these preconditions.

Many international agreements fail one or both of these tests. Some of the agreements negotiated during the Uruguay Round can be cited in this connection. Consider, for example, the international agreement on trade-related aspects of intellectual property rights (TRIPs), which sets minimum standards of protection in patents, copyrights, and trademarks, and the agreement on trade-related investment measures (TRIMs), which requires the phasing out of performance requirements such as local-content and export-import linkage requirements. These represent cases of "forced" harmonization despite the absence of convincing evidence of benefits to developing nations. TRIPs is a particularly egregious instance, in that what the governments of the developed countries really obtained was the transfer of billions of dollars' worth of monopoly profits from poor countries to rich countries under the guise of protecting the property rights of inventors.[6] The draft Multilateral Agreement on Investment, which was under negotiation until recently at the OECD, contains many other doubtful restrictions on policy actions.

Some of the proposals to link the strengthening of labor standards in developing countries to trade privileges are problematic from the same perspective. In principle, there is nothing wrong with the international community requiring developing-country governments to protect basic worker rights. At times, this simply amounts to requiring that governments live up to commitments they have already made in the relevant International

Labour Organisation (ILO) conventions they have ratified, such as those on the freedom of association and the minimum working age. The freedoms to associate and to organize are basic civil rights, and there is some evidence, as I have shown in previous chapters, that such freedoms are associated with superior economic performance. But often the demands from labor advocates in the developed countries go beyond basic civil rights and political liberties, and prescribe outcomes that may lead to inferior economic performance. The requirement that workers in developing countries be paid a "living wage" or the implementation of specific prohibitions on child labor may well end up doing more harm than good. The argument for international discipline is considerably weaker in such instances.[7]

The proposal to enshrine capital-account convertibility in the IMF's Articles of Agreement is another idea that lacks empirical justification. If recent evidence teaches us anything, it is that there is a compelling case for maintaining controls on short-term borrowing. The three countries hardest hit by the Asian financial crisis—Indonesia, Thailand, and South Korea—were the three in the region with the largest short-term obligations (in relation to reserves or exports). It is not that capital controls are necessarily the remedy for boom-and-bust cycles in international financial markets; they are not. But capital-account liberalization fills the bill even less. We can imagine cases in which the judicious application of capital controls could have prevented a crisis or greatly reduced its magnitude. Thailand and Indonesia would have been far better off restricting borrowing from abroad than encouraging it. South Korea just might have avoided a run on its reserves if controls on short-term borrowing had kept its short-term exposure to foreign banks, say, at 30 percent of its liabilities, rather than 70 percent.

Admittedly, we know too little about what kinds of controls work best in these circumstances. The evidence on the effectiveness of controls on short-term borrowing is patchy. But incomplete knowledge of this sort is an argument for allowing countries to follow their own preferred paths, selecting their own trade-offs between risk and reward.

A common argument in favor of capital market integration is that this serves to discipline governments, forcing them to follow sound fiscal and monetary policies. For governments with a penchant for populist macroeconomic policies, such market discipline can serve a useful role, much the same way that tariff bindings under the WTO help prevent excessive responsiveness to lobbying by industry groups at home. But this argument can be taken too far. In most democratic societies, the discipline needed by governments is provided by electoral accountability and by a constitutional system of checks and balances. Governments that mess up the economy are punished at the polls. It is not at all clear that international markets systematically improve the incentives faced by democratic governments. Certainly, the availability of financial resources on easy terms during periods of market euphoria can encourage fiscal profligacy—rather than penalize it—and result in quite the opposite effect. Moreover, market discipline empowers financial markets—domestic and foreign—over other constituencies in society, creating serious problems for democratic governance. Hence, in practice, the potential value of market discipline has to be traded off against the downside risks.

In sum, policymaking at the international level has to create space for national development efforts that are divergent in their philosophy and content. Forcing all countries into a single, neoliberal developmental model would be unwise—in light of the potential political backlash from national groups—even if there were serious grounds to believe that the model is economically advantageous. It is absurd when the evidence on the model's economic superiority is itself in doubt.

The lesson of history is that ultimately all successful countries develop their own brand of national capitalism. As Alexander Gerschenkron (1965) demonstrated, the patterns of development during the nineteenth century were quite diverse, and more recent economic history provides little evidence of convergence. The United States, Sweden, Germany, and Japan, to name just a few instances, are alike in that they are market-based economies that uphold private property and monetary stability. But the economic systems in these countries also differ on many important dimensions, including the organization of the labor market, the style of corporate governance, the extent of social insurance and safety nets, the intrusiveness of the government, and the regulatory framework in product and labor markets. Developing countries can choose among these and, no doubt, many other paths; they should be left free to do so.

· ·

A QUESTION OF ACCOUNTABILITY

■   THE INTERNATIONALIZATION OF PRODUCTION and investment raises a fundamental question of accountability: to whom will national economic policymakers be accountable? The implicit answer provided by the globalization model is that they will be accountable to foreign investors, country-fund managers in London and New York, and a relatively small group of domestic exporters. In the globalized economy, these are the groups that determine whether an economy is judged a success or not, and whether it will prosper.

This would not necessarily be a bad thing if the invisible hand of global markets could always be relied upon to produce desirable outcomes. The reality is considerably more murky. It takes too much blind faith in markets to believe that the global allocation of resources is enhanced by the twenty-something-year- olds in London who move hundreds of millions of dollars around the globe in a matter of an instant, or by the executives of multinational enterprises who make plant location decisions on the basis of the concessions they can extract from governments. As Eatwell (1997) points out in reference to financial markets:

> If the financial markets are simply enforcing the logic of real economic efficiency, strengthening the self-adjusting powers of competitive markets, then the "disciplining" of governments would be benign, but if markets are pursuing the rules of a beauty contest and imposing self-fulfilling prejudices on the workings of the real economy, then the outcome may be very damaging . . . . When [markets'] influence is combined with the persistent search for government "credibility," defined in terms of "sound money" and "prudent" deflationary policies, then the [low-growth, high-unemployment equilibrium] is the most likely outcome. (pp. 246-247)

These words, written before the Asian and Russian crises, are remarkably prescient in light of what has come to pass since 1997.[8]

What is wrong, therefore, with the first chapter's parable of the fictional finance minister is that the minister is spending the vast majority of his time worrying about how the rest of the world evaluates his management of the economy. Traditional developmental concerns have been all but squeezed out. For this minister, it is global markets that dictate policy, not domestic priorities.

The fundamental dilemma of accountability in today's world economy is that it is domestic voters who choose national governments—and appropriately so—and not global markets. International markets, particularly financial ones, do not always get things right with respect to economic efficiency. They are even less likely to get things right with regard to societal outcomes suitable to each nation's aspirations. The structure of social institutions in a country, the extent of inequality that is tolerated, the types of public goods to be provided by governments—these are issues that are, and should be, resolved at the national level. Choices about social arrangements will vary across nations because of differences in norms, historical traditions, and levels of development. It is national governments that are held responsible for producing outcomes that are consonant with national aspirations. If governments can no longer be responsive to these aspirations, they can no longer be accountable to their electorates.

It may be true, as the conventional wisdom has it, that the information revolution and the globalization of production necessitate novel forms of governance. We need to figure out what these forms of governance are and how we can institute them. But national governments are all we have at present. It would be unwise to give them up without knowing what will replace them. A suitable international economic system is one that allows different styles of national capitalism to coexist with each other—not one that imposes a uniform model of economic governance.

NOTES

[1] The Martian is smart enough to realize that richer countries—regardless of growth rate—have fewer restrictions on trade in goods and capital, and she controls for that.

[2] It bears repeating the reasons why this finding departs from the conventional wisdom, especially given that conventional wisdom appears to be grounded in a large number of empirical studies. One reason is that many of the leading studies confound the trade regime with an economy's macroeconomic stability by using measures that are based on black-market premiums or exchange rates. When more appropriate indicators, that is, tariff and nontariff barriers to trade, are substituted for these hybrid measures, the strong results typically vanish. A second reason is that some studies use measures of openness that are based on actual volumes of trade or foreign investment. The results from these studies are uninformative on the role of openness because countries that grow fast also tend to experience rapid growth in trade and are more attractive to foreign investors.

[3] See also Mosley (1998), which underscores many of the same findings, including the nonrobust relationship between trade policy and growth and the insignificance of government size in long-run performance.

[4] On evidence that tariffs may have speeded up growth in the late 19th century, see O'Rourke (1997).

[5] Information obtained from the IMF Web site. See http://www.imf.org/External/np/exr/facts/asia.htm (Box 4) and http://www.imf.org/external/np/oth/korea.htm.

[6] The most direct consequence of the TRIPs agreement is an increase in prices of items such as pharmaceuticals for which patent treatment in the developing nations has been traditionally weak. The magnitude of the price increase one can expect is indicated by an exercise carried out by Subramanian (1994), who compares the prices for patented drugs in Malaysia (where patent protection for pharmaceuticals is reasonably tight) with those in India (where it is not). He finds that Malaysian prices are significantly higher than Indian ones, with the premium ranging from 17 percent (for Pentoxyphyllin 400 mg tablets) to 767 percent (for Atenolol 50 mg tablets). Insofar as the owners of patents in such drugs are foreign-owned firms (as is the case almost always), developing countries are faced not only with monopoly distortions in the home market, but, more important, with a potentially huge transfer of rents abroad.

[7] Indeed, the United States has ratified very few of the ILO's conventions, citing the U.S. federal structure (and the role of the states in regulatory policy) and other special circumstances.

[8] And not only in East Asia. Developing-country governments all over the world have had to tighten credit for fear of losing their credibility in international financial markets. "Brazil Pays to Shield Currency, and the Poor See the True Cost," was the headline of a *New York Times* article (authored by Roger Cohen) on February 5, 1998.

Appendix

Most of the data used in this book come from three sources: the Penn World Tables (Mark 5.6), the World Bank's data files (World Bank 1995, 1997b), and the Barro and Lee (1994) data set. Depending on the period covered and the purpose of the analysis, real per capita incomes and investment rates are taken either from the Penn World Tables (which are adjusted for purchasing power) or from the World Bank data files (which are not).

WORLD BANK COUNTRY CODES

Countries in the scatter plots are identified by their World Bank country codes. The country codes are listed below.

CODE	Country	CCODE	CODE	Country	CCODE
1	Algeria	DZA	16	Gambia	GMB
2	Angola	AGO	17	Ghana	GHA
3	Benin	BEN	18	Guinea	GIN
4	Botswana	BWA	19	Guinea-Bissau	GNB
5	Burkina Faso	HVO	20	Côte d'Ivoire	CIV
6	Burundi	BDI	21	Kenya	KEN
7	Cameroon	CMR	22	Lesotho	LSO
8	Cape Verde	CPV	23	Liberia	LBR
9	Central African Rep.	CAF	24	Madagascar	MDG
10	Chad	TCD	25	Malawi	MWI
11	Comoros	COM	26	Mali	MLI
12	Congo	COG	27	Mauritania	MRT
13	Egypt	EGY	28	Mauritius	MUS
14	Ethiopia	ETH	29	Morocco	MAR
15	Gabon	GAB	30	Mozambique	MOZ

CODE	Country	CCODE	CODE	Country	CCODE
31	Niger	NER	78	Venezuela	VEN
32	Nigeria	NGA	79	Afghanistan	AFG
33	Rwanda	RWA	80	Bahrain	BHR
34	Senegal	SEN	81	Bangladesh	BGD
35	Seychelles	SYC	82	Myanmar (Burma)	BUR
36	Sierra Leone	SLE	83	China	CHN
37	Somalia	SOM	84	Hong Kong	HKG
38	South Africa	ZAF	85	India	IND
39	Sudan	SDN	86	Indonesia	IDN
40	Swaziland	SWZ	87	Iran, I.R. of	IRN
41	Tanzania	TZA	88	Iraq	IRQ
42	Togo	TGO	89	Israel	ISR
43	Tunisia	TUN	90	Japan	JPN
44	Uganda	UGA	91	Jordan	JOR
45	Zaire	ZAR	92	Korea	KOR
46	Zambia	ZMB	93	Kuwait	KWT
47	Zimbabwe	ZWE	94	Malaysia	MYS
48	Bahamas	BHS	95	Nepal	NPL
49	Barbados	BRB	96	Oman	OMN
50	Canada	CAN	97	Pakistan	PAK
51	Costa Rica	CRI	98	Philippines	PHL
52	Dominica	DMA	99	Saudi Arabia	SAU
53	Dominican Rep.	DOM	100	Singapore	SGP
54	El Salvador	SLV	101	Sri Lanka	LKA
55	Grenada	GRD	102	Syria	SYR
56	Guatemala	GTM	103	Taiwan	OAN
57	Haiti	HTI	104	Thailand	THA
58	Honduras	HND	105	United Arab Emirates	ARE
59	Jamaica	JAM	106	Yemen, N.Arab	YEM
60	Mexico	MEX	107	Austria	AUT
61	Nicaragua	NIC	108	Belgium	BEL
62	Panama	PAN	109	Cyprus	CYP
63	St. Lucia	LCA	110	Denmark	DNK
64	St. Vincent & Grens.	VCT	111	Finland	FIN
65	Trinidad & Tobago	TTO	112	France	FRA
66	United States	USA	113	Germany, West	DEU
67	Argentina	ARG	114	Greece	GRC
68	Bolivia	BOL	115	Hungary	HUN
69	Brazil	BRA	116	Iceland	ISL
70	Chile	CHL	117	Ireland	IRL
71	Columbia	COL	118	Italy	ITA
72	Ecuador	ECU	119	Luxembourg	LUX
73	Guyana	GUY	120	Malta	MLT
74	Paraguay	PRY	121	Netherlands	NLD
75	Peru	PER	122	Norway	NOR
76	Suriname	SUR	123	Poland	POL
77	Uruguay	URY	124	Portugal	PRT

CODE	Country	CCODE
125	Spain	ESP
126	Sweden	SWE
127	Switzerland	CHE
128	Turkey	TUR
129	United Kingdom	GBR
130	Yugoslavia	YUG
131	Australia	AUS
132	Fiji	FJI
133	New Zealand	NZL
134	Papua New Guinea	PNG
135	Solomon Islands	SLB
136	Tonga	TON
137	Vanuatu	VUT
138	Western Samoa	WSM

References

Aghevli, Bijan, and Jorge Marquez-Ruarte. 1985. *A Case of Successful Adjustment: Korea's Experience During 1980-84.* IMF Occasional Paper 39. Washington, DC: IMF.

Akyuz, Yilmaz, and Charles Gore. 1994. "The Investment-Profits Nexus in East Asian Industrialization." UNCTAD Discussion Paper 91 (October).

Amsden, Alice H. 1989. *Asia's Next Giant: South Korea and Late Industrialization.* New York: Oxford University Press.

Aslund, Anders, Peter Boone, and Simon Johnson. 1996. "How to Stabilize? Lessons from Post-Communist Countries." *Brookings Papers on Economic Activity* 1:217-291.

Aw, Bee Yan, Sukkyun Chang, and Mark J. Roberts. 1998. "Productivity and Turnover in the Export Market: Micro Evidence from Taiwan and South Korea." Pennsylvania State University, processed (March).

Baker, Dean, Gerald Epstein, and Robert Pollin, eds. Forthcoming 1998. *Globalization and Progressive Economic Policy: What Are the Real Constraints and Options?* New York: Cambridge University Press.

Balassa, Bela, and associates. 1971. *The Structure of Protection in Developing Countries.* Baltimore, MD: The Johns Hopkins University Press.

Barkan, Joel, and David Gordon. 1998. "Democracy in Africa," *Foreign Affairs* (July/August): 107-111.

Barro, Robert J. 1996. "Determinants of Economic Growth: A Cross-Country Empirical Study." NBER Working Paper 5698 (August). Cambridge, MA: National Bureau for Economic Research.

Barro, Robert, and Jong-Wha Lee. 1994. "Data Set for a Panel of 138 Countries." Cambridge, MA: Harvard University. (January).

Bell, Daniel A. 1998. "After the Tsunami: Will Economic Crisis Bring Democracy to Asia?" *The New Republic* (March 9, 1998): 28.

Bernard, Andrew B., and J. Bradford Jensen. 1998. "Exporting and Productivity." Paper presented at the 1998 Summer Institute, NBER, Cambridge, MA, August 1998.

———. 1995. "Exporters, Jobs, and Wages in U.S. Manufacturing, 1976-1987" *Brookings Papers on Economic Activity: Microeconomics 1995*: 67-112.

Bhalla, Surjit S. Forthcoming. "Freedom and Economic Growth: A Virtuous Cycle?" In *Democracy's Victory and Crisis: Nobel Symposium 1994*, ed. Axel Hadenius. New York: Cambridge University Press.

Bigsten, Arne, et al. 1998. "Exports and Firm-Level Efficiency in the African Manufacturing Sector." (July). World Bank. Unpublished.

Bijan Aghevli and Jorge Marquez-Ruarte. 1985. "A Case of Successful Adjustment: Korea's Experience During 1980-84." IMF Occasional Paper 39. Washington, DC: IMF.

Blomstrom, Magnus, Robert E. Lipsey, and Mario Zezan. 1996. "Is Fixed Investment the Key to Economic Growth?" *Quarterly Journal of Economics* CXI (February): 269-276.

Bosworth, Barry, and Susan Collins. 1998. "Capital Inflows, Investment, and Growth." (October). Washington, DC: Brookings Institution.

Brautigam, Deborah. 1997. "Institutions, Economic Reform, and Democratic Consolidation in Mauritius." *Comparative Politics* 30(1) (October): 45-62.

Brecher, Richard, and Carlos Diaz-Alejandro. 1977. "Tariffs, Foreign Capital and Immiserizing Growth." *Journal of International Economics* 7: 317-322.

Bruton, Henry J. 1998. " A Reconsideration of Import Substitution." *Journal of Economic Literature* XXXVI (June): 903-936.

Celasun, Merih, and Dani Rodrik. 1989. "Debt, Adjustment, and Growth: Turkey." Book IV in *Developing Country Debt and Economic Performance: Vol. 3, Country Studies— Indonesia, Korea, Philippines, Turkey*, ed. J. Sachs and S. Collins. Chicago: University of Chicago Press.

Chadra, Siddharth. 1998. "On Pillars of Democracy and Economic Growth," Graduate School of Public and International Affairs, University of Pittsburgh. (February).

Clerides, Sofronis, Saul Lach, and James Tybout. 1998. "Is 'Learning-by-Exporting' Important? Micro-Dynamic Evidence from Colombia, Mexico, and Morocco." *Quarterly Journal of Economics* CXIII(3) (August): 903-47.

Coe, David T., and Alexander W. Hoffmaister1998. "North-South Trade: Is Africa Unusual?" IMF Working Paper. (June). Washington, DC: IMF.

Cohen, Daniel. 1997. "Growth and External Debt: A New Perspective on the African and Latin American Tragedies." CEPREMAP Discussion Paper No. 9715. (July). Paris.

Cohen, Roger. 1998. "Argentina Grapples with the Downside of Globalization." *The New York Times* (February 6, 1998).

Collier, Paul. 1998. "The Political Economy of Ethnicity." Paper prepared for the Annual World Bank Conference on Development Economics, Washington, DC, April 20-21.

———. 1995. "The Marginalization of Africa." *International Labour Review* 134(4-5): 541-57.

Collins, Susan, and Barry Bosworth. 1996. "Economic Growth in East Asia: Accumulation Versus Assimilation." *Brookings Papers on Economic Activity* 2: 135-91.

Cummings, Bruce. 1998. "South Korea's Challenge." *In These Times* 22(6) (February 22): 15.

Dean, Judith M., Seema Desai, and James Riedel. 1994. "Trade Policy Reform in Developing Countries Since 1985: A Review of the Evidence." World Bank Discussion Paper 267. Washington, DC: World Bank.

Deininger, Klaus, and Lyn Squire. 1996. "A New Data Set Measuring Income Inequality." *The World Bank Economic Review* (September): 565-91.

de Long, J.B., and L.H. Summers. 1991. "Equipment Investment and Economic Growth." *Quarterly Journal of Economics* 106: 445-502.

Dominguez, Jorge I. 1998. "The Relationship Between Democracy and Open Markets." Harvard University. Unpublished. (April).

———. 1997. "Latin America's Crisis of Representation." *Foreign Affairs*, (January/February): 100-13.

Easterly, William. 1997. "The Ghost of Financing Gap." World Bank. Unpublished. (July).

———. 1993. "How Much Do Distortions Affect Growth?" *Journal of Monetary Economics* 32(2): 187-212.

Easterly, William, and Ross Levine. 1997. "Africa's Growth Tragedy: Policies and Ethnic Divisions." *Quarterly Journal of Economics* CXII (November): 1203-50.

Eatwell, John. 1997. "International Capital Liberalization: The Impact on World Development." *Estudios de Economia* 24(2) (December): 219-61.

The Economist. 1998a. "Asian Pride: Dollars and Dolours." (January 24): 38.

———. 1998b. "Oppression in Indonesia: Taking the Blame." (February 28): 46.

Elbadawi, Ibrahim. 1998. "Real Exchange Rate Policy and Non-Traditional Exports in Developing Countries." Nairobi: African Economic Research Consortium. (June).

Feenstra, Robert. 1990. "Trade and Uneven Growth." NBER Working Paper 3276. Cambridge, MA: NBER.

Feenstra, Robert, and Gordon Hanson. 1996. "Foreign Investment, Outsourcing and Relative Wages." In *The Political Economy of Trade Policy: Papers in Honor of Jagdish Bhagwati*, ed. R. Feenstra, G. Grossman, and D. Irwin. Cambridge, MA, MIT Press.

Feldstein, Martin. 1998. "Refocusing the IMF." *Foreign Affairs* (March/April).

Financial Times (London). 1998. "Union Calls Off General Strike." (February 14): 2.

Fischer, Stanley. 1998. "In Defense of the IMF." *Foreign Affairs* (July/August): 103-106.

Fischer, Stanley, Ratna Sahay, and Carlos Vegh. 1996. "Stabilization and Growth in the Transition Economies: The Early Experience" *Journal of Economic Perspectives* 10(2) (Spring): 45-66.

Frank, Charles R., Jr., Kwang Suk Kim, and Larry Westphal. 1975. *Foreign Trade Regimes and Economic Development: South Korea.* New York: Columbia University Press.

Gerschenkron, Alexander. 1965. *Economic Backwardness in Historical Perspective: A Book of Essays.* New York: Praeger.

Frankel, Jeffrey A., and David Romer. 1996. "Trade and Growth: An Empirical Investigation." NBER Working Group Paper 5476. Cambridge, MA: NBER. (March).

Grossman, Gene, and Elhanan Helpman. 1991. *Innovation and Growth in the Global Economy*. Cambridge, MA: MIT Press.

Gulhati, Ravi. 1990. *The Making of Economic Policy in Africa*. Washington, DC: Economic Development Institute, World Bank.

Hadjimichael, M.T., M. Nowak, R. Sharer, and A. Tahari. 1996. *Adjustment for Growth: The African Experience*. Washington, DC: International Monetary Fund. (October).

Hadjimichael, M.T., T. Rumbaugh, and E. Verreydt. 1992. *The Gambia: Economic Adjustment in a Small Open Economy*. Washington, DC: International Monetary Fund. (October).

Hagopian, Frances. 1998. "Negotiating Economic Transitions in Liberalizing Polities: Political Representation and Economic reform in Latin America." Weatherhead Center for International Affairs Working Paper Series No. 98-5. Harvard University. (May).

Harrison, Ann. 1996. "Determinants and Effects of Direct Foreign Investment in Côte d'Ivoire, Morocco, and Venezuela." In *Industrial Evolution in Developing Countries*, ed. Mark J. Roberts and James R. Tybout. New York: Oxford University Press.

Harrold, Peter. 1995. "The Impact of the Uruguay Round on Africa." World Bank Discussion Papers 311. Washington, DC: World Bank.

Harvey, Charles. 1992. "Botswana: Is the Miracle Over?" *Journal of African Economies* 1(3), (November): 335-68.

Harvey, Charles, and Stephen R. Lewis, Jr. 1990. *Policy Choice and Development Performance in Botswana*. London: Macmillan.

Hein, Philippe. 1989. "Structural Transformation in an Island Country: The Mauritius Export Processing Zone." *UNCTAD Review* 1(2): 41-58.

Helleiner, Gerry K. 1997. "Africa in the Global Economy." University of Toronto. Unpublished. (May).

———1995. "Introduction." In *Manufacturing for Export in the Developing World : Problems and Possibilities*, ed. Helleiner. London: Routledge.

Helliwell, John,. 1994. "Empirical Linkages Between Democracy and Economic Growth." *British Journal of Political Science* XXIV: 225-48.

Hellman, Joel S. 1998. "Winners Take All: The Politics of Partial Reform in Postcommunist Transition." *World Politics* 50(2) (January): 203-34.

Institute of International Finance (IIF). 1998. "Capital Flows to Emerging Market Economies." (January 29).

Jacoby, Sanford. 1998. "Risk and the Labor Market: Societal Past as Economic Prologue." Institute of Industrial Relations Working Paper No. 98-02. Los Angeles: UCLA.

Jaggers, K., and T. R. Gurr. 1995. "Tracking Democracy's Third Wave with Polity III Data." *Journal of Peace Research* 32: 469-82.

Jones, Leroy, and Il Sakong. 1980. *Government, Business, and Entrepreneurship in Economic Development: The Korean Case*. Cambridge, MA: Harvard University Press.

Knack, Stephen, and Philip Keefer. 1995. "Institutions and Economic Performance: Cross-Country Tests Using Alternative Institutional Measures." *Economics & Politics* (November): 207-28.

Kolodko, Grzegorz W. 1998. "Equity Issues in Policymaking in Transition Economies." Paper presented at Conference on Economic Policy and Equity, IMF, Washington, DC, June 8-9, 1998.

Krueger, Anne. 1993. *Political Economy of Policy Reform in Developing Countries.* Cambridge, MA, MIT Press.

Kuo, Shirley. 1983. *The Taiwan Economy in Transition.* Boulder, CO: Westview Press.

Landes, David. 1998. *The Wealth and Poverty of Nations.* New York: W.W. Norton.

Larimer, Tim, Terry McCarthy, and Chuan Leekpai. 1998. *Time* (March 30): 16.

Lawrence, Robert Z. 1996. *Regionalism, Multilateralism, and Deeper Integration.* Washington, DC: Brookings Institution.

Levine, Ross, and David Renelt. "Sensitivity Analysis of Cross-Country Growth Regressions." *American Economic Review* 82 (September): 942-63.

Lewis, Stephen R., Jr. 1993. "Policymaking and Economic Performance: Botswana in Comparative Perspective." In *Botswana: The Political Economy of Democratic Development*, ed. Stephen John Stedman. Boulder, CO: Lynne Rienner Publishers.

Lin, Ching-yuan. 1973. *Industrialization in Taiwan, 1946-72: Trade and Import-Substitution Policies for Developing Countries.* New York: Praeger.

Little, Ian M.D., et al. 1993. Boom, Crisis, and Adjustment: The Macroeconomic Experience of Developing Countries. New York: Oxford University Press for the World Bank.

Little, Ian M.D., Tibor Scitovsky, and Maurice Scott. 1970. *Trade and Industry in Some Developing Countries.* New York: Oxford University Press.

Lora, Eduardo, and Juan Luis Londono. 1998. "Structural Reforms and Equity." In *Beyond Trade-Offs: Market Reform and Equitable Growth in Latin America*, ed. N. Birdsall, C. Graham, and R.H. Sabot. Washington, DC: Brookings Institution Press.

Maddison, Angus. 1985. *Two Crises: Latin America and Asia: 1929-38 and 1973-83, Development Centre Studies.* Paris: OECD.

Matsuyama, Kiminori. "Agricultural Productivity, Comparative Advantage, and Economic Growth." *Journal of Economic Theory* 58(2) (December): 317-34.

Mauro, Paolo. 1995. "Corruption and Growth." *Quarterly Journal of Economics* (August): 681-712.

Meade, James E., et al. 1961. *The Economics and Social Structure of Mauritius—Report to the Government of Mauritius* London: Methuen.

Meller, Patricio. 1995. "Chilean Export Growth, 1970-90." In *Manufacturing for Export in the Developing World: Problems and Possibilities*, ed. G. K. Helleiner. London: Routledge.

Milner, Chris, and Andrew McKay. 1996. "Real Exchange Rate Measures of Trade Liberalization: Some Evidence for Mauritius." *Journal of African Economies* 5(1): 69-91.

Mosley, Paul. 1998. "Globalization and Policy Reforms: Another Look at the IMF Approach to Future Developing Country Growth." University of Reading, Studies on International Monetary and Financial Issues for the G-24. (September).

O'Donnell, Guillermo. 1979. "State and Alliances in Argentina, 1956-76." *Journal of Development Studies*.

OECD. 1997. *The World in 2020*. Paris, OECD.

O'Rourke, Kevin. 1997. "Tariffs and Growth in Late Nineteenth Century." CEPR Discussion Paper 1700. (October).

Pissarides, Christopher. 1997. "Learning by Trading and the Returns to Human Capital in Developing Countries." *The World Bank Economic Review* 11(1) (January): 17-32.

Pritchett, Lant, and Daniel Kaufmann. 1998. "Civil Liberties, Democracy, and the Performance of Government Projects." *Finance & Development* (March): 26-29.

Przeworski, Adam, and Fernando Limongi. 1993. "Political Regimes and Economic Growth." *The Journal of Economic Perspectives* VII (Summer): 51-69.

Quinn, Dennis P., and John T. Woolley. 1998. "Democracy and National Economic Performance: The Search for Stability." School of Business, Georgetown University. (June).

Radelet, S. 1993. "The Gambia's Economic Recovery: Policy Reforms, Foreign Aid, or Rain?" *Journal of Policy Modeling* 15(3): 251-276.

Radelet, Steve, and Jeffrey Sachs. 1998. "The Onset of the Asian Financial Crisis." Harvard University. Unpublished.

Rahul, Jacob. 1998. "Back from the Dead." *Time*, February 16, p.21.

Robinson, James A. 1997. "Political Equilibrium and Free Trade." University of Southern California. (October).

Rodrik, Dani. Forthcoming 1998a. "TFPG Controversies, Institutions and Economic Performance in East Asia." In *The Institutional Foundation of Economic Development in East Asia*, ed.Y. Hayami and M. Aoki. London: Macmillan.

———. 1998b. "Where Did All the Growth Go? External Shocks, Social Conflict, and Growth Collapses." NBER Working Paper. (January).

———. Forthcoming 1998c. "Why Is Trade Reform So Difficult in Africa?" *The Journal of African Economies* 7(2).

———. 1997a. "Democracy and Economic Performance." John F. Kennedy School of Government, Harvard University. (December).

———. 1997b. *Has Globalization Gone Too Far?* Washington, DC: Institute for International Economics.

———. 1997c. "Trade Policy and Economic Performance in Sub-Saharan Africa." Harvard University. Paper prepared for the Division of International Cooperation of the Ministry for Foreign Affairs, Sweden. (November).

———. 1997d. "Trade Strategy, Exports, and Investment: Another Look at East Asia." *Pacific Economic Review* (February).

———. 1996a. "Coordination Failures and Government Policy: A Model with Applications to East Asia and Eastern Europe." *Journal of International Economics* 40(1-2) (February): 1-22.

———. 1996b. "Understanding Economic Policy Reform." *Journal of Economic Literature* XXIV (March): 9-41.

———. 1995a. "Developing Countries After the Uruguay Round." In UNCTAD, *International Monetary and Financial Issues for the 1990s*, Vol. VI. New York: United Nations.

———. 1995b. "Getting Interventions Right: How South Korea and Taiwan Grew Rich." *Economic Policy* 20.

———. 1995c. "Trade and Industrial Policy Reform." In *Handbook of Development Economics*, Vol. III, ed. Jere Behrman and T. N. Srinivasan. Amsterdam: North-Holland.

Romer, Paul. 1994. "New Goods, Old Theory, and the Welfare Costs of Trade Restrictions." *Journal of Development Economics* 43: 5-38.

———. 1993. "Two Strategies for Economic Development: Using Ideas and Producing Ideas." In *Proceedings of the World Bank Annual Conference on Development Economics 1992*. Washington, DC: World Bank.

Rowthorn, Robert, and Richard Kozul-Wright. 1998. "Globalization and Economic Convergence: An Assessment." UNCTAD Discussion Paper 131. Geneva: UNCTAD. (February).

Sachs, Jeffrey, and Andrew Warner. 1997. "Sources of Slow Growth in African Economies." Harvard Institute for International Development. (March).

———. 1995. "Economic Reform and the Process of Global Integration." *Brookings Papers on Economic Activity* 1: 1-118.

Sahn, D.E., ed. 1994. *Adjusting to Policy Failure in African Economies*. Ithaca: Cornell University Press.

Samuelson, Robert J. 1998. "Global Capitalism, R.I.P?" *Newsweek* (September 14, 1998): 40.

Simonsen, Mario Henrique. 1988. "Price Stabilization and Incomes Policy: Theory and the Brazilian Case Study." In *Inflation Stabilization: The Experience of Israel, Argentina, Brazil, Bolivia, and Mexico*, ed. Michael Bruno et al. Cambridge, MA: MIT Press.

Ssemogerere, G. 1997. "Trade Liberalization in Uganda, 1981-1995: Episodes, Credibility and Impact on Economic Development, with a Sample Survey of Enterprises Manufacturing Tradeables." Submitted to the AERC Project on Trade Liberalization and Regional Integration. (February).

Stiglitz, Joseph. 1998. "Knowledge and Development: Economic Science, Economic Policy, and Economic Advice." Paper prepared for the Annual World Bank Conference on Development Economics, Washington, DC, April 20-21, 1998.

Subramanian, Arvind. 1994. "Putting Some Numbers on the TRIPs Pharmaceutical Debate." *International Journal of Technology Management* 10(10).

Taylor, Alan. 1997. "Argentina and the World Capital Market: Saving, Investment, and International Capital Mobility in the Twentieth Century." NBER Working Paper 6302. Cambridge, MA: NBER. (December).

———. 1996. "On the Costs of Inward-Looking Development: Historical Perspectives on Price Distortions, Growth and Divergence in Latin America from the 1930s to the 1980s." NBER Working Paper 5432. (Cambridge, MA. (January).

Temple, Jonathan. 1998. "Equipment Investment and the Solow Model." *Oxford Economic Papers* 50: 39-62.

Temple, Jonathan, and Paul A. Johnson. 1998. "Social Capability and Economic Growth." *Quarterly Journal of Economics* CXIII (August): 965-90.

Tsiang, S.C. 1984. "Taiwan's Economic Miracle: Lessons in Economic Development." In *World Economic Growth*, ed. Arnold C. Harberger. San Francisco, CA: Institute for Contemporary Studies Press.

Tutu, K. A. and A. D. Oduro. 1996. "Trade Liberalization in Ghana." Report on Trade and Regional Integration Presented to the African Economic Research Consortium. (March).

UNCTAD. 1994. *Directory of Import Regimes, Part I: Monitoring Import Regimes.* New York: United Nations.

Vernon, Raymond. 1988. *In the Hurricane's Eye: The Troubled Prospects of Multinational Enterprises.* Cambridge, MA: Harvard University Press.

Wade, Robert. 1990. *Governing the Market: Economic Theory and the Role of Government in East Asian Industrialization.* Princeton, NJ: Princeton University Press.

Wellisz, Stanislaw, and Philippe Lam Shin Saw. 1993."Mauritius." In *The Political Economy of Poverty, Equity, and Growth: Five Open Economies*, ed. Ronald Findlay and Stanislaw Wellisz. New York: Oxford University Press.

Woochan. 1997. "Does Capital Account Liberalization Discipline Budget Deficits?" John F. Kennedy School of Government, Harvard University.

Wood, Adrian. 1997. "Openness and Wage Inequality in Developing Countries: The Latin American Challenge to East Asian Conventional Wisdom." *The World Bank Economic Review* 11(1) (January): 33-57.

Wood, Adrian, and Jorg Mayer. 1998. "Africa's Export Structure in Comparative Perspective." UNCTAD, Geneva, unpublished paper. (April).

World Bank. 1998. *World Development Report 1998.* Washington, DC: World Bank.

———. 1997a. *Global Economic Prospects and the Developing Countries.* Washington, DC: World Bank.

———. 1997b. *World Development Indicators 1997.* Washington, DC: World Bank.

———. 1996a. *Trends in Developing Economies, 1996.* Washington, DC: World Bank.

———. 1996b. *Uganda: The Challenge of Growth and Poverty Reduction.* Washington, DC: World Bank.

———. 1995. *World Data 1995* [CD-ROM]. Washington, DC: World Bank.

———. 1993. *The East Asian Miracle: Economic Growth and Public Policy.* New York: Oxford University Press for the World Bank.

World Trade Organization. 1995. *Trade Policy Review: Uganda.* (October).

Yeats, Alexander with Azita Amjadi, Ulrich Eincke, and Francis Ng. 1997. *Did Domestic Policies Marginalize Africa in World Trade?* Directions in Development Series. Washington, DC: World Bank.

Young, Alwyn. 1995. "The Tyranny of Numbers: Confronting the Statistical Realities of the East Asian Growth Experience." *Quarterly Journal of Economics* CX(3) (August): 641-680.

———. 1992. "A Tale of Two Cities: Factor Accumulation and Technical Change in Hong Kong and Singapore." In *NBER Macroeconomics Annual*, ed. O. Blanchard and S. Fischer. Cambridge, MA: MIT Press.

About the Author

DANI RODRIK is Professor of International Political Economy at the John F. Kennedy School of Government, Harvard University, and Senior Advisor at the Overseas Development Council. He is also a Research Associate of the National Bureau of Economic Research and a Research Fellow of the Centre for Economic Policy Research. He is author of *Has Globalization Gone Too Far?* (Institute for International Economics 1997); co-author of *Emerging Agenda for Global Trade* (ODC 1996); co-author of *Miracle or Design? Lessons from the East Asian Miracle* (ODC 1994); and author of many articles on international economics, economic development, and political economy in professional journals.

About the ODC

The Overseas Development Council (ODC) is an independent, international policy research institution based in Washington, DC, that seeks to improve decision making on multilateral cooperation in order to promote more effective development and the better management of related global problems. Its program focuses on the interrelationship of globalization and development, and improved multilateral responses to these linked challenges.

To this end, ODC provides analysis, information, and evaluation of multilateral policies, actions, and institutions; develops innovative ideas and new policy proposals; and creates opportunities for decision makers and other interested parties to participate in discussions of critical global issues and decisions.

ODC is governed by an international Board of Directors of recognized and widely respected policy leaders on multilateral development and global issues. Peter D. Sutherland is its Chairman, and John W. Sewell is ODC's President.

ODC is a private, nonprofit organization, funded by foundations, governments, and private individuals.

O | D | C

OVERSEAS DEVELOPMENT COUNCIL
1875 CONNECTICUT AVENUE, NW
SUITE 1012
WASHINGTON, DC 20009
TEL. 202-234-8701
FAX 202-745-0067
http:\\www.odc.org

POLICY ESSAY NO. 24

ODC Board of Directors